Better Homes and Gardens®

orchid gardening

Houghton Mifflin Harcourt

Boston New York

Better Homes and Gardens® Orchid Gardening

Contributing Writer: Ellen Zachos
Contributing Project Editor: Deb Wiley
Contributing Designers: Sundie Ruppert, Lori Gould
Editor, Garden Books: Denny Schrock
Editorial Assistant: Heather Knowles
Contributing Copy Editor: Fran Gardner
Contributing Proofreaders: Fern Marshall Bradley, Terri Fredrickson
Contributing Indexer: Ellen Sherron
Contributing Photographers: Doug Hetherington,
   Dean Schoeppner, Denny Schrock
Contributing Photo Manager: Deb Wiley
Contributing Photo Researcher: Susan Ferguson

Meredith® Books

Editorial Director: Gregory H. Kayko
Editor in Chief, Garden: Doug Jimerson
Art Director: Tim Alexander
Managing Editor: Doug Kouma
Executive Director, Sales: Ken Zagor
Director, Operations: George A. Susral
Business Director: Janice Croat
Contributing Imaging Center Operator: Ryan Alexander

Publisher: Natalie Chapman
Associate Publisher: Jessica Goodman
Executive Editor: Anne Ficklen
Assistant Editors: Charleen Barila, Meaghan McDougall
Production Director: Diana Cisek
Manufacturing Manager: Tom Hyland

This book is printed on acid-free paper.

Copyright © 2011 by Meredith Corporation, Des Moines, IA.
All rights reserved.

Published by Houghton Mifflin Harcourt Company.
Published simultaneously in Canada.

For information about permission to reproduce selections from this book, write to trade.permissions@hmhco.com or to Permissions, Houghton Mifflin Harcourt Publishing Company, 3 Park Avenue, 19th Floor, New York, New York 10016.

Note to Reader: Due to differing conditions, tools, and individual skills, Meredith Corporation assumes no responsibility for any damages, injuries suffered, or losses incurred as a result of following the information published in this book. Before beginning any project, review the instructions carefully, and if any doubts or questions remain, consult local experts or authorities. Because codes and regulations vary greatly, you should always check with authorities to ensure that your project complies with all applicable local codes and regulations. Always read and observe all the safety precautions provided by manufacturers of any tools, equipment, or supplies, and follow all accepted safety procedures.

Better Homes and Gardens® Magazine
Editor in Chief: Gayle Goodson Butler

Meredith Publishing Group
President: Tom Harty
Excutive Vice President: Doug Olson

Meredith Corporation
President and Chief Executive Officer: Stephen M. Lacy

Photo Credits
Photographers credited may retain copyright © to the listed photographs.
Curtis's Botanical Magazine (1862, vol. 88, public domain photo): 17L, Ellen Zachos: 134R, 135, 138TL, 141TR, 141BL, 142TL, 145TL, 147TL, 148TL, 150TR, 160BR, 173BR, 182BR, 190BR, 174TL, 195TL, 196TR, 199BL, 202BR, 203TL, 203TR, 212R

Library of Congress Cataloging-in-Publication Data available on request

ISBN 978-0-470-93028-1

2010042156

Printed in China
SCP 10 9 8 7 6 5 4 3 2
4500681779

mysterious and breathtakingly lovely, orchids bring brightness, color, and joy to your home. Use the inspiring images and easy-to-follow advice to choose, plant, grow, and care for these precious bloomers.

table of contents

P G131

Glossary

Common orchid terms

As with other types of gardening, orchids come with their own specific vocabulary. Here are some definitions to help you as you learn more about growing these tropical beauties.

ALLIANCE
A group of related orchids that shares certain characteristics and cultural needs, named after the most prominent genus in the group, such as the cattleya alliance, the oncidium alliance, or the vanda alliance

BACKBULBS
Old pseudobulbs that eventually lose their foliage and are no longer in active growth

CANE
A thick stem that produces foliage and flower spikes, and stores reserves of water and nutrition

EPIPHYTE
A plant that grows on another plant; takes no nutrition from its host, but merely uses it for anchorage

GENUS
A biological classification of orchids within an alliance that shares common characteristics; the plural is genera

GREX
The hybrid offspring of two orchid species; appears as the second part of the hybrid orchid's name, following the genus

INTERGENERIC
A hybrid between or among two or more orchid genera

KEIKI
A baby orchid that grows as an offshoot from mature plants

LITHOPHYTE
A plant that grows on rocks; usually highly drought tolerant

MONOPODIAL
A plant with a single growing point; one stem that grows taller with age

NOID
No identification; an orchid that is unlabeled or unidentified beyond the genus

NOTHOGENUS
A genus that does not occur in nature; made by crossing two or more genera to develop a new genus

PSEUDOBULBS
Specialized storage tissues for water and food; may be oval, cylindrical, or round and produce foliage and flower spikes

RHIZOME
An underground stem that produces roots and stems; sympodial orchids grow along horizontal rhizomes

SYMPODIAL
A plant with new growth emerging laterally from preceding growth

TERRESTRIAL
A plant that grows on the ground; some with roots that penetrate soil, but others with shallow roots that grow through a lightweight layer of moss and leaf litter

history & exploration

From ancient Greece to Victorian England, orchids were collected for their magical and medicinal properties and admired as symbols of romance and exotic beauty.

p.10
ORCHID HISTORY

Orchids come with a romantic, exotic, and even dangerous history, wrapped in intrigue and myth. They've been used as food and assigned magical properties of fertility and grace.

p.18
NEW ORCHID DEVELOPMENT

Orchid seeds are so tiny it's almost impossible for the average home gardener to work with them. Luckily, professional growers can start orchids for gardeners.

p.20
UNDERSTANDING ORCHID NAMES

Just a little botanical Latin helps you easily understand a plant's name. That's important in helping select and grow the exact orchid you want.

Orchids through the ages

The stunning red-orange blooms of *Phragmipedium besseae* originally hail from Ecuador and Peru.

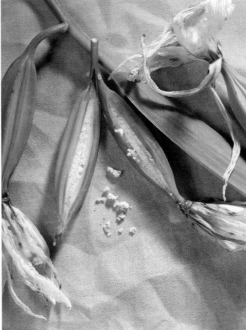

Botanists used to believe orchids were newly evolved

because they had found no fossilized plants. That misconception cleared up in 2007 when orchid pollen was discovered on a 20 million-year-old bee fossil.

Why was it so hard to find fossilized orchids? Generally, orchids have soft tissues and grow in warm, moist conditions that lead to quick biodegradation. Millions of years ago, a fallen orchid was much more likely to decay than to fossilize. Orchid seeds are tiny (as fine as baby powder), and the pollen degrades readily in the acid used to clean fossils.

It all goes to show that orchids are not only fascinating and alluring, they are a lot tougher than they look.

Orchids survived the dinosaurs

The history of orchids spans millions of years and six continents. It's believed the first orchids appeared about 80 million years ago but began to flourish only after the mass extinction that wiped out the dinosaurs approximately 65 million years ago. (No more giant dinosaur feet trampling tiny orchids!)

A cataclysmic prehistoric event may have wiped out *Tyrannosaurus rex*, but the dainty orchid soldiered on.

Fast forward a few million years to China in the 28th century BC. Legend says the mythical Emperor Shennong had two orchids in his medical encyclopedia: a bletilla and a dendrobium.

In the fifth century BC, Confucius dubbed the orchid "King of Fragrant Plants," and numerous Chinese writings used orchids as symbols for all that was refined, noble, elegant, and feminine.

Elsewhere in Asia, the fragrance of *Cymbidium ensifolium* was credited with magical powers. In Japanese folklore, the childless wife of a Japanese emperor gave birth to 13 children after breathing in the orchid's scent.

Magical powers of fertility?

Theophrastus (371–287 BC) left the first written record of orchids in Western literature, describing in great detail how they could be used as aphrodisiacs and to either increase or decrease fertility. When Victorian scholars translated his classic text *Enquiry Into Plants*, they left out this section; it was deemed too racy and offended their delicate sensibilities.

Ancient Greeks and Romans considered the orchid a symbol of virility and fertility. Dioscorides, a Greek physician practicing medicine in Rome, described in *De Materia Medica* (65 AD) the bulbous roots of several terrestrial orchids native to the Mediterranean. The tubers grew in pairs, one firm and full, the other soft and shriveled. Dioscorides claimed that if a woman ate the small, soft tuber, she would have a daughter; if her husband ate the large, firm tuber, she would have a son.

Above left: **Dendrobium atroviolaceum 'Pygmy' × 'Little Elf' is a modern dendrobium hybrid.**

Above center: **Orchid seeds are minuscule—about the size of a grain of flour—making them difficult for home gardeners to propagate.**

Above right: **Bletilla was one of the two orchids mythical Chinese Emperor Shennong included in his medical encyclopedia of the 28th century BC.**

Orchids through the ages

You can grow *Vanilla planifolia* for its culinary pods, but it takes so long to mature and set fruit that it's easier to use the tendrils of a variegated vanilla vine as a living wreath.

In the late Middle Ages, salep, made from dried and ground orchid tubers, was a popular flavor in the Ottoman Empire. Today, you can still eat orchid ice cream in Turkey and other parts of the Arab world and drink hot salep beverage served from samovars. Unfortunately, tons of orchid tubers are wild-collected every year to make these products, and the orchids are now endangered.

Halfway around the globe, Totonac natives of Mexico harvested the seedpods of the climbing orchid *Vanilla planifolia* to use as a perfume, aphrodisiac, and healing herb.

The Aztecs used *V. planifolia* to stave off mental and physical fatigue and to flavor their delicious cacao drink.

Cortez found the taste of vanilla compelling and brought it home to Spain, where its popularity spread rapidly throughout Europe.

Modern scientists synthesized vanilla flavor, and today you can find both pure and artificial vanilla extract on supermarket shelves. Most shoppers never learn the origin of the flavor.

Orchids in literature

In *Hamlet*, written around 1600, Shakespeare referred to orchids as "long purples" and "dead men's fingers" in the drowned Ophelia's bouquet.

In 1653, Nicholas Culpeper described them in his comprehensive herbal texts as being "under the dominion of Dame Venus." He warned they could "provoke lust exceedingly" and were "hot and moist in operation."

It was official: Orchids were sexy and dangerous.

In early 20th-century France, Marcel Proust used cattleya orchids as symbols of lust in *Remembrance of Things Past*. Just a few years later, in Depression-era New York City, Nero Wolfe, the hero of Rex Stout's classic American detective novels, compared his hothouse orchids to expensive, temperamental concubines.

How did orchids get their name?

An ancient Greek myth tells the story of Orchis, the son of a satyr and a nymph. Orchis insulted a priestess of Dionysus (the god of wine) and, for that crime, was killed by the god's drunken followers. Orchis's father convinced Dionysus to turn his son into a flower—an orchid.

TEST GARDEN TIP

Orchids and evolution

Darwin speculated about coevolution by observing an *Angraecum sesquipedale* orchid and a moth. In his theory, the orchid's fragrance attracts the moth, which inserts its proboscis into the 11½-inch nectary. Pollen deposited on the moth's head is carried to another flower. A moth with a shorter proboscis couldn't reach the nectar, and a flower with a shorter nectary couldn't align pollen with the head of a long-tongue moth. They evolved together, allowing both to reproduce.

Left: **Orchids make outstanding cut flowers, lasting for about a week. Keep blooms cool and away from direct sunlight.**

Below: **Cymbidiums (below) or cattleyas are often used as lapel or wrist corsages.**

Orchid history

By the end of the 18th century, European interest in orchids as ornamentals had begun to blossom. Wealthy amateur botanists and public gardens funded explorations to tropical climates in search of exotic plants that would win fame and horticultural honors. One of the hunters was Captain William Bligh who brought cargoes of tropical orchids from Australia, the West Indies, and Jamaica back to England several years after the mutiny on the HMS *Bounty*.

One enthusiastic British botany sponsor was William Cattley, who received an unassuming-looking orchid plant from Brazil in 1818. Legend has it that these orchids were so unremarkable that they were used merely as packing material for more obviously captivating plants.

Above: **Some orchids hail from tropical rain forests where humidity and temperatures remain high. That's why those types suffer in the dry, temperate atmosphere of most homes.**

When that orchid bloomed in Cattley's greenhouse, the flower's size, color, and fragrance ignited a passion among British botanists that became known as orchidelirium. The plant was named *Cattleya labiata* after the man who paid for the expedition rather than for William Swainson, the naturalist who risked life and limb to obtain the captivating plant.

Darwin and the orchid controversy

Hunting rare tropical plants was a glamorous and dangerous profession during the mid-19th century, a golden age of plant exploration. Glass manufacturing had improved enough to make greenhouse growing productive. Botanic gardens enthusiastically received a rush of exotic plant material discovered in distant lands, and naturalists and botanists avidly studied the new acquisitions.

Charles Darwin was one of those naturalists. He spent years studying the form and function of tropical orchids. In 1862 he wrote a book about their fertilization and pollination: *Fertilisation of Orchids by Insects.* Darwin theorized that the flower of *Angraecum sesquipedale*, with its 11½-inch-long nectar-producing gland, must be pollinated by a moth with a similarly long proboscis.

He suggested that these two species had coevolved in a synergistic relationship. This idea aggravated his contemporaries who didn't believe in evolution. With this discussion, the sensual orchid became both theologically provocative and scientifically relevant.

In 1905, 23 years after Darwin's death, the existence of the Morgan's sphinx moth, which has a 12-inch-long proboscis, was confirmed in Madagascar.

What's in a name?

Orchids are often named for their discoverers (*Phalaenopsis micholitzii* for William Micholitz), those who paid for their discovery (*Vanda sanderiana* for Frederick Sander), or European botanists who studied and described the orchids.

John Lindley (1799–1865), a British botanist known as the father of modern orchidology, described almost 2,000 orchid species. Each carries his name after the botanical name, such as *Oncidium cavendishianum* Lindley (or Lindl).

Today's orchids still amaze

Successful propagation and hybridization made orchids widely available at reasonable prices by the end of the 1800s.

By that time, the Philadelphia nurseryman A. Blanc was offering orchids at 50 cents each or 12 for $5. Even adjusted for inflation, those are rock-bottom prices.

Today orchids are considered ornaments, botanical status symbols, and gorgeous living bouquets. But orchids still have practical uses in cultures around the globe. Australian aborigines use cymbidium orchids as cures for dysentery as well as for contraception. In Africa, orchids are used as food and to treat stomach and fertility problems. In modern Western medicine, vanilla improves food intake and reduces nausea in chemotherapy patients.

There's certainly nothing wrong with a sweet smell and a pretty face. But the next time you're in the plant department, admiring blooms of so many shapes and colors, remind yourself that the beauty of orchids runs more than skin deep.

Above top: **Angraecum sesquipidale**, also known as Darwin's orchid, has a long nectar-producing gland that attracts a specific moth for pollination.

Above: **Discovered by explorers in 1818, *Cattleya labiata* was ignored—until it bloomed. The beautiful flower was named for British expedition sponsor William Cattley.**

Orchid exploration

Albert Millican, in his 1891 book

Travels and Adventures of an Orchid Hunter, described the hazards of the hunt:

"I was delighted to find the trees on the rising ground from the banks of the river hung with fine clumps of *Miltonia vexillaria*, intermixed with *Oncidium carthagenense* and several smaller orchids, and I was priding myself upon reaping a glorious harvest. But that night all my plans were destined to be crushed. Everybody was in good spirits at our evening meal, but we had scarcely finished and lighted our roll of tobacco when the twang of an arrow, as it whistled past my head, startled everyone to his feet. In another moment one of our number was pierced with three of the deadly poisoned arrows, and mortally wounded."

Today you need only go online or to a garden center to find orchids. But 200 years ago, plant explorers were rock stars who combined danger with beauty, and travel with discovery.

Above: **Orchid displays captivate today's viewers as they did the early explorers—in much safer surroundings.**

ASK THE GARDEN DOCTOR

What's a Wardian case?

ANSWER: A mid-19th century London physician and amateur botanist, Nathaniel Ward, noticed that fern spores germinated readily in closed glass cases. His discovery gave rise to Wardian cases, glass containers that allowed people to grow sensitive plants in their homes. The cases greatly improved the survival rate of orchids and other tropical treasures on their long journeys from native habitats to Europe.

Sadly, many of them met untimely ends in faraway places. George Skinner died of yellow fever in Panama (1867), Gustav Wallis succumbed to dysentery in the Andes (1878), and David Burke's body was found in a tribesman's hut in the Molucca Islands (1897).

Thomas Lobb, discoverer of *Vanda coerulea*, was lucky to lose only a leg while exploring in the Philippines for tropical treasures.

A cold-blooded quest

In the 19th century, commercial nurseries in Europe sent collectors to Central and South America, India, Madagascar, and Papua New Guinea. It wasn't unusual for several orchid collectors to show up in the same place at the same time, looking for the same orchids.

When that happened, they didn't play fair. Hunters were known to strip locations of all orchids, even if they didn't want them, just so no one else could have them. Their employers encouraged this often-ruthless competition.

William Arnold, one of the most famous orchid hunters of the Victorian era, was en route to Caracas, Venezuela, on behalf of London nurseryman Frederick Sander when he recognized a fellow traveler as a hunter working for Sander's rival, John Lowe. The two men, heavily armed, barely avoided a duel. When Arnold reported the altercation, Sander encouraged Arnold to spy on the competition.

Another of Sander's hunters, William Micholitz, found a trove of *Dendrobium phalaenopsis* growing among skulls and human bones. The plants sold immediately, but Micholitz refused to return for more, claiming he had no desire to leave his own skull behind.

Still hunting orchids

Building an orchid collection today is a lot less dangerous than it was in the 19th century, but there are still many intrepid hunters out there, searching for new species in out-of-the-way places.

CITES (the Convention on International Trade in Endangered Species of Wild Fauna and Flora) regulates international transport of orchids. Originally conceived to protect wild populations of plants and animals from decimation by trade, CITES is considered a mixed blessing in some circles.

While the treaty prohibits wholesale collection of orchids from their natural habitats, it also prevents the export of plants rescued from areas scheduled to be burned, flooded, or bulldozed.

Without income potential, local inhabitants have no motivation to salvage these plants, and whole populations of plants are being lost. Because rescued plants could be propagated by cloning, a single plant transported to a nursery or lab could produce hundreds of copies, preserving the species rather than destroying it.

Above left: **Early botanical prints feature exotic-looking orchids such as paphiopedilums.**

Above right: **Wardian cases not only look attractive, but they also can serve as miniature greenhouses for orchids—as long as the plants are given good air circulation.**

New orchid development

Rhyncholaeliocattleya Dick Smith 'Paradise' is an intergeneric hybrid nothogenus, resulting from a cross of a rhyncholaelia and a cattleya.

Today's new orchids are mostly the result of hybridization

and laboratory work, although species are still discovered in nature. In 2002, the discovery of *Phragmipedium kovatchii* in Peru and its subsequent transport to Florida made headlines. But questions about the legality of its importation resulted in fines for the importer and resignations from the botanical garden that published the orchid description.

Nonetheless, most orchids today are not wild-collected but grown in nurseries or produced in labs. Hand-pollination is possible, but orchid seeds are so fine—resembling dust—that they're difficult to work with. There was little in the written record about orchid seed until the 19th century because the seeds were so hard to spot. Orchid reproduction was swathed in mystery.

Most orchids produce vast quantities of seeds, but few germinate. In the late 1800s, botanists got some seeds to grow by planting them at the base of a parent plant. Scientists understood that the parent plant contained something crucial for seed germination, but they didn't know what it was.

In 1899, French biologist Noel Bernard confirmed the symbiotic relationship between orchid seeds and the mycorrhizal fungus *Rhizoctonia*, present in the growing medium surrounding the parent orchids' roots.

Cracking the key to orchid germination

Most familiar (and much larger) garden seeds contain enough food reserves to nourish themselves during germination. However, tiny orchid seeds contain almost no endosperm.

In nature, *Rhizoctonia* fungi penetrate the seed, providing it with the nutrition necessary for germination. In the lab, Bernard successfully inoculated orchid seeds with the fungus. He began to experiment with applying nutrients directly to the seeds, but died before he was able to prove his theory.

At Cornell University in 1922, Louis Knudson germinated seeds on sterile media in flasks with a nutrient solution. This revolutionized commercial orchid growing and made a wide variety of plants available at more-affordable prices.

Mass-producing orchids

Growing orchids from seeds produces a crop of related, but not identical plants. For orchid hybridizers, the process of seed propagation is essential since it's the only way to combine desirable traits of parent orchids. But once the perfect plant has been generated, how can a commercial grower produce more exactly like it?

Mericloning is a propagation technique that guarantees each young plant is identical to the parent plant. It's a kind of tissue culture (also called micropropagation) and can be done only under sterile conditions. Tissue is taken from the parent plant and minced into tiny pieces that are grown to maturity under sterile laboratory conditions.

When an orchid is deemed exceptional, it's propagated by mericloning so its remarkable traits (scent, flower size, color, and so forth) can be reliably continued. Because this is a more expensive process than growing from seed, mericlones can cost more than seed-grown plants. Buyers pay extra to know exactly what they're getting.

Mericloned orchids are grown just like traditional hybrids or species. The fact that they were vegetatively propagated in a lab makes no difference in their cultural requirements.

While it's possible for the dedicated amateur to hybridize orchids at home and to grow plants from seed, it's unlikely most hobbyists would invest the time and money to practice micropropagation.

Some tissue culture laboratories produce mericlones from plant tissue submitted by individual growers. So when you create the next wonderful orchid hybrid in your hobby greenhouse, you can order flasks of mericlones to sell for fun and profit.

ASK THE GARDEN DOCTOR

What's a NOID?

ANSWER: The abbreviation NOID means no identification. A dendrobium NOID is a dendrobium identified only to the level of genus. For example, you may see *Dendrobium speciosum* or *Dendrobium* sp. (sp. is the abbreviation for species.) Both of these indicate the dendrobium is a species (not a hybridized grex) but that the species is unknown.

Below left: **To create orchids that exactly resemble the parent plant, tiny pieces of tissue are propagated (mericloned) in flasks.**

Below right: **Because it doesn't live in the wild where pollinators can do the job, this yellow cattleya must be pollinated by hand.**

Understanding orchid names

Botanical Latin can seem intimidating.

The most important reason to use the botanical name for a plant is to get exactly what you want, because common names vary from place to place. With orchids, nomenclature is even more important. Plants with similar names can be surprisingly different. If you want to be sure you get what you ask for, it pays to learn how to identify the orchid by its complete and correct botanical name.

Start with the genus

Every orchid name has at least two parts. Let's break it down into manageable bites and start with the genus, the first part. (The plural is genera.) A genus is a group of plants classified together due to common ancestry and shared characteristics. The group can be naturally occurring or manmade. When written, the genus of a plant's name is capitalized and either italicized or underlined.

Related genera can interbreed to create new hybrids. These are called intergeneric hybrids. Their names may be written in several ways. An intergeneric hybrid of two different genera is usually created by combining the names of the original genera. For example, a hybrid between a *Cattleya* and a *Brassia* is a *Brassocattleya* orchid, often abbreviated as Bc.

An intergeneric hybrid combining three genera may be created by combining the names, as in *Brassocatanthe* (*Brassavola* × *Cattleya* × *Guarianthe*, abbreviated Bct.) or by creating a new genus name ending in –ara. For example, *Aliceara* is an intergeneric hybrid of *Brassia*, *Miltonia*, and *Oncidium*.

Any intergeneric hybrid combining four or more genera is always given a new genus name, also ending in –ara. An example is a *Volkertara*, a hybrid of *Broughtonia*, *Cattleya*, *Guarianthe*, and *Rhyncholaelia*.

The term nothogenus is used to describe a manmade genus; *Volkertara* is a nothogenus. You may see an "×" in front of an intergeneric hybrid name, as in × *Volkertara*. This indicates it is a cross between two or more genera.

What the second part means

The second part of an orchid name may be either a species or a grex name.

A species (also known as the specific epithet) is a group of closely related plants within a genus. A species occurs naturally. Like a genus name, a species name should be italicized or underlined. It is not capitalized. A species name tells you something about the plant. It may indicate flower color (*coccinea* means red in Latin), place of origin (*philippense* means it originated in the Philippines), or who discovered the orchid (*micholitzii* means associated with Micholitz).

Like orchid genera, orchid species can be hybridized. If species hybridize naturally, the resulting plant may be given a new species name.

Above: **Until recently this orchid was a *Vuylstekeara*, but it's now a *Miltonidium* due to name changes of the parent genera. The grex name remains Fall in Love, and the cultivar name is 'Lovely Lady'.**

TEST GARDEN TIP

How to write orchid names

When written, the first mention of each genus is completely spelled out. After that, the genus name can be abbreviated according to the official list of orchid abbreviations published by the Royal Horticultural Society in London. While there are rules for how to correctly write orchid names, you often see them written incorrectly, not capitalized or italicized. Remember, even professionals make mistakes. For a list of abbreviations of orchids in this book, see page 133.

Paphiopedilum × *siamense* is the natural cross of *P. callosum* × *P. appletonianum*. Sometimes the parents' names are listed (in addition to or instead of a new species name), especially if the parent orchids are well known and considered valuable. The female parent is always listed first.

What's a grex name?

When two species are hybridized by a grower, the hybrid offspring are given a group name, or grex. The grex name is capitalized, but not underlined or italicized. Orchids that share a grex name may look quite different from one another, just as human siblings do.

Cultivar names

If a plant is special, it may be given a cultivar name. A cultivar is a single genetic representation of a species or hybrid. Cultivar names are capitalized, enclosed within single quotation marks, and not underlined or italicized. Once registered, cultivars are vegetatively propagated so their desirable characteristics are passed to the next generation.

String together a genus, a grex, and a cultivar, and you get a long orchid name. But the time and effort put into hybridizing top-quality plants mean that growers need to be clear about what they're selling.

Dissecting a name

If you ask for an epicatt you'll get an epicatt. But how do you guarantee you'll get a multiflowered epicatt with linear green petals and a wildly colorful lip of yellow and magenta? The only way is to ask for it by its full (and complicated!) name: *Epicattleya* René Marqués 'Tyler'.

Epicattleya is an intergeneric hybrid of *Epidendrum* and *Cattleya*. It could also be written

× *Epicattleya*. *Epicattleya* is a nothogenus and is abbreviated as Epc.

René Marqués is a grex name. All the orchid offspring of *Epidendrum pseudepidendrum* and *Cattleya claesiana* share René Marqués as their grex name.

'Tyler' is a cultivar name that was registered because somebody somewhere thought this particular offspring was truly special. It has been vegetatively propagated and is a clone of the original 'Tyler' cultivar.

Names do change

Orchid nomenclature is a fluid topic. Taxonomists change earlier classifications when technology provides updated information. They move orchids from one genus to another and create entirely new genera.

For example, what was a *Potinara* two years ago is now called something else. *Potinara* was a combination of *Cattleya*, *Brassavola*, *Laelia*, and *Sophronitis*. The genus *Sophronitis* has been totally eliminated, as have several of the species within the other three contributing genera. What was once a species within the genus *Potinara* may now be a species within any of several genera. You have to trace back the individual parentage; there is no single answer.

In the Gallery of Orchids starting on page 130 every effort has been made to use the most up-to-date names, but growers sometimes take a while to catch up. Earlier names are also listed if they're still likely to be seen on plant tags.

For the most up-to-date classifications, check the Royal Horticultural Society database (*http://apps.rhs.org.uk/horticulturaldatabase*).

Above left: **Robert's Delight 'Torblue' is a vanda with the grex name Robert's Delight and cultivar name 'Torblue'.**

Above right: **Robert's Delight 'Garnet Beauty' is a vanda orchid with the grex name Robert's Delight and cultivar name 'Garnet Beauty'. You can see the relationship to Robert's Delight 'Torblue'.**

form & function

Orchids belong to one of the largest plant families on Earth. As with any big family, its members can look very different from one another. Still, they have more in common than you might think.

p.24
WHAT IS AN ORCHID?

There are about 25,000 species from about 900 genera, and more than 100,000 hybridized hybrids and cultivars. But all of them share certain traits.

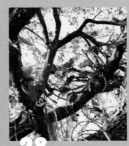

p.28
WHERE ORCHIDS GROW

Orchids grow on different kinds of surfaces. It's important to know whether your orchid is terrestrial (growing on the ground), lithophytic (on rocks), or epiphytic (with aerial roots on other plants).

p.30
ORCHID PARTS

Each part of an orchid gives you a clue about how it likes to grow. The types of roots and leaves it has, and whether it grows with pseudobulbs or canes, all indicate something about what the orchid likes best.

p.34
HOW TO "READ" AN ORCHID

You can tell a lot about an orchid just by looking at it. Now that you know how orchids grow, you can begin to learn the differences among the many genera.

What makes an orchid an orchid?

Some orchids, such as *Paphiopedilum* Hsinying Carlos, produce a single giant, glorious flower.

Orchids are known as either the biggest plant family

(Orchidaceae) or second in size to the daisy family (Asteraceae), depending on your source. Whether first or second, however, there are lots of orchids out there: about 25,000 species from about 900 genera, and that's not counting more than 100,000 manmade hybrids and cultivars.

Orchids grow on six of the seven continents, but the greatest variety and concentration, by far, come from the tropics. This book focuses on tropical orchids since they are best suited as houseplants.

So, what makes an orchid an orchid? What do all these thousands of plants have in common that makes them more like one another than like any other flowering plants?

Orchids share common traits

In the 18th century, Carl von Linné (Linnaeus) developed a method of categorizing plants according to their reproductive parts. All orchid flowers (which are the reproductive parts) have several things in common: the pistils and stamens are fused into a column, they are bilaterally symmetrical, and one petal (the lip, also known as the labellum) is highly modified.

You might not immediately realize that a giant paphiopedilum flower is related to the dwarf bloom of *Haraella odorata*, but it is.

A new way to classify orchids

Modern technology and the ability to perform DNA analysis on plant tissues have given rise to a new system of classification: cladistics. Instead of grouping plants by their reproductive parts, cladistics groups them according to ancestry. In other words, a group consists of an ancestor and all its descendants. This group is called a clade. Think of it as a branch on a family tree.

Cladistics originated in the mid-20th century and at first was based on shared morphological characteristics, somewhat similar to the Linnean system of classification.

Today, DNA analysis is often used to generate cladograms. Groups are still defined according to shared characteristics, but cladistics focuses on characteristics derived from common ancestry rather than those that evolved separately.

The result of this scientific shift is that taxonomists make frequent changes to botanical names as they shift organisms from one genus to another. One example is the disappearance of the genus *Sophronitis*.

The plant itself hasn't changed, but all the plants within the genus have been moved into *Cattleya*.

Does this change how you grow the plant? It does not. Instead of looking for *Sophronitis coccinea*, you'll now shop for *Cattleya coccinea*. But if you see *Soph. coccinea* on a plant tag, that's still the plant you want.

TEST GARDEN TIP

Choosing fragrance

Orchids with strong perfumes usually rely on scent rather than flashy petals to attract pollinators. Orchids often have specific pollinator relationships. When its pollinator is most active, an orchid is usually most fragrant. Orchids with white flowers (*Brassavola nodosa, Angraecum* species) are fragrant and visible at night to attract certain moths. Cattleyas are more fragrant during the day when their pollinators—bees and flies—are active.

Above: **Orchids with white flowers, such as *Brassavola nodosa*, are more fragrant at night, when the moths that pollinate them are active.**

Left: **Some types of orchids, such as phalaenopsis, can produce multiple flowers on each bloom spike.**

Parts of a flower
Each type of orchid looks a bit different on the outside but they all share a common structure.

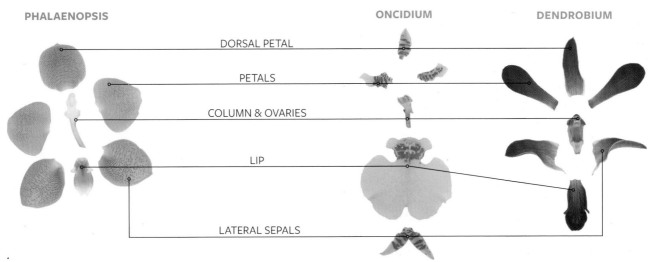

PHALAENOPSIS · ONCIDIUM · DENDROBIUM

DORSAL PETAL
PETALS
COLUMN & OVARIES
LIP
LATERAL SEPALS

Speaking orchid

Slipper orchids, such as
Paphiopedilum petula
'Orlando', are sympodial
orchids—when they grow,
they form a new plant
beside the old one.

To truly understand orchids, you need to speak their language.

That includes two important terms from the botanical lexicon describing the growth habits of orchids: monopodial and sympodial. Understanding the difference helps you better pot and propagate your plants.

Monopodial orchids have a single growing point; the word is from Greek, meaning "one-footed." Monopodial orchids grow from a single stem that increases in height with age.

Examples are phalaenopsis, vanda, and angraecum orchids. They cannot be divided to make more plants.

Sympodial orchids have multiple growing points. The word sympodial comes from Greek, meaning "with joined feet." Sympodial orchids grow horizontally, with new growth emerging laterally from earlier growth. They increase in diameter with age.

Examples of sympodial orchids are cattleyas, oncidiums, and dendrobiums. Any large sympodial specimens can be divided to make more orchids.

TEST GARDEN TIP

Sympodials or monopodials?

Paphiopedilums and phragmipediums may look like monopodial orchids, but they aren't. They produce new foliage next to their existing leaves, not on top of them. If you look closely at the crown of your plant, you'll see each new group of leaves creates another growing point, making these sympodial orchids.

Above top: **This paphiopedilum (slipper orchid) is sympodial, growing new leaves along one side.**

Above bottom: **The monopodial growth habit of a phalaenopsis shows leaves growing on top of one another, from a single growing point.**

A phalaenopsis orchid is monopodial, with a single growing point rising from the roots.

Where orchids grow

This cattleya is an epiphytic orchid; its large roots are attached to a tree.

Orchids grow on different types of surfaces (also called

substrates) and are considered either terrestrial, lithophytic, or epiphytic.

Knowing where your orchid grows in nature gives you essential information on how to care for your plant at home.

Epiphytes are the types of tropical orchids most people grow in their homes. The word means "upon a plant" and in nature, epiphytes grow on other plants. However, they are not parasites; they take no nutrition from their host plants.

Instead, they use aerial roots (roots not covered with substrate) to anchor themselves above the ground in the plant canopy where foliage receives more light than it would below.

Their roots, exposed to the air, absorb rain. Debris from the trees above (insects, dead leaves) provides occasional nutrition. Epiphytic types encompass most of the orchids in this book, such as phalaenopsis, oncidium, cattleya, and vanda.

Terrestrial tropical orchids grow on the ground but they don't necessarily grow in the ground. They grow in the top layer of fluffy moss and leaf litter of a rain forest floor rather than in heavy soil. Their roots are thick, shallow, and covered with water-absorbent hairs.

Terrestrial orchids in rain forest locations are highly shaded by the tree canopy. Indoors, these orchids tolerate lower light levels than most epiphytes.

Terrestrial types include cymbidium, phragmipedium, and paphiopedilum orchids.

Lithophytes (literally, rock-plants) are similar to epiphytes, but instead of growing on trees, they grow on rocks. Roots anchor them in place and may draw nutrition from cracks and crevices where debris has fallen.

Lithophytic orchids generally require high humidity and frequent drenching. They include some dendrobium and laelia species.

Left: **Terrestrial orchids include the genus *Phaius*, shown here as *Phaius* 'Joan Hart'. This orchid prefers shade and plenty of moisture.**

Above: **Lithophytic orchids, such as *Pleione formosana*, can attach their roots to rocky surfaces.**

Roots matter

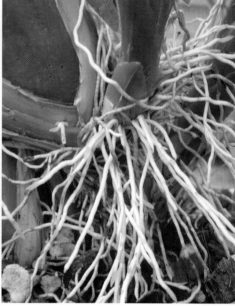

Ephiphytic and lithophytic orchids have specialized

roots that hold them in place. These aerial roots are thick, fleshy, and covered with a substance called velamen.

Velamen is a spongy layer of dead cells that absorbs water quickly. For roots exposed to brief but frequent rain showers, this is a useful characteristic. Velamen also slows the loss of water from root tissue by evaporation.

In nature, velamen roots are exposed to frequent cycles of wetness and drying. In the home, it's essential that velamen roots be well aerated so they can dry rapidly. If they are surrounded by moist soil, they quickly rot.

While terrestrial orchid roots don't have a velamen layer, they do have a water-absorbent, hairy surface. These roots are generally shallow and penetrate the top layers of humus and debris on the rain forest floor. They are not as fully exposed to the air as epiphytic orchid roots, but neither are they constantly surrounded by moist soil.

Keep orchids out of soil

Most houseplants grow well in a lightweight potting mix, either soilless or soil-based. But most orchids should be grown in bark mix to give the plants' roots what they need: a balanced exposure to water and air.

Traditional potting mix is fine-grain and retains moisture around a plant's root ball. While this is great for many houseplants, it can be deadly for orchids. Velamen absorbs moisture quickly from a brief rainstorm or even highly humid air. If velamen is kept constantly moist (as it would be if surrounded by moist potting mix), it rots, and the orchid dies.

Epiphytic and lithophytic orchids should be grown in bark mix for excell   drainage. Some terrestrial orchids also need bark mix to mimic the texture of the fluffy top layer of moss and humus of the forest floor.

Terrestrial rain forest orchids aren't necessarily growing in soil, although they are growing on the ground. A few tropical terrestrial orchids, including most jewel orchids, grow well in a soilless potting mix (such as a peat-based mix), like the rest of your houseplants.

Above left: **After watering, phalaenopsis roots appear green as the velamen absorbs moisture.**

Above right: **The aerial roots on some types of orchids resemble fine white strings.**

Opposite: **The roots of many orchids, including phalaenopsis, grow outside their pots, seeking air and moisture.**

Leaves, canes, & pseudobulbs

Red Emperor 'Prince' dendrobium grows its magenta blooms from canes shaped like spindles. This type commonly loses its leaves during flowering.

Some orchid leaves are thick and fleshy while others are thin and papery.

All are covered by a cuticle—a waxy, protective layer produced by a leaf's epidermis. The cuticle slows the loss of water through the leaf's surface and also protects leaf tissue from bacteria and other disease organisms.

The thickness of the cuticle varies from plant to plant and is often a good indicator of drought tolerance. An orchid with shiny, stiff, smooth leaves has a thick cuticle that helps retain moisture. An orchid with paper-thin, pliable leaves has a thinner cuticle and loses water more quickly.

Canes and pseudobulbs

A pseudobulb is a unit of specialized storage tissue for water and food that is found on some sympodial orchids. In nature, an orchid's pseudobulbs are plump and full during the rainy season. They may become depleted and wrinkled during the dry season when the orchid draws upon the food and water reserves stored inside.

Leaves and flowers grow from active pseudobulbs. As new bulbs emerge on a sympodial orchid, older pseudobulbs lose their foliage and are considered backbulbs. Backbulbs may not be in active growth, but they are still important as storage tissue. They may also contain dormant buds that can be coaxed into growth via division.

Canes are straight, thick stems that produce foliage and flower spikes from obvious, regular nodes. They serve a purpose similar to pseudobulbs: to store food and water for the plant.

Above: **Oncidium orchids grow with large, fleshy pseudobulbs rising above the roots.**

Below: **Cut leaves from a phalaenopsis, left, and a paphiopedilum show the difference in leaf thickness.**

How to "read" an orchid

Now that you've learned the language of orchid structure, you can

tell a lot about your plant just by looking at it. Here are a few examples:

Vanda

A vanda is an epiphyte. Its numerous thick velamen roots hold it in place on a host tree where it receives strong light.

What does that tell you about how a vanda might grow best in your home?

For optimum exposure to the air, vanda roots should be potted in a coarse, lightweight bark mix or not potted at all. They are often sold as bark-mounted specimens or simply held in open-worked baskets that allow constant air circulation to the roots.

Vandas require high light intensity. In nature they grow high in the canopy in relatively unobstructed sunlight. In your home they need full sun exposure.

Above: **Robert's Delight 'Royale Show' vanda is a high-light orchid that needs plenty of air circulation.**

Paphiopedilum

A paphiopedilum is a terrestrial slipper orchid. Its roots are thick and spongy compared with traditional garden plants, but less so than the roots of an epiphytic orchid. The paphiopedilum's leaves are thin and pliable.

Because paphiopedilum leaves don't have a thick cuticle, they lose moisture more quickly than leaves with substantial waxy coverings. Thus, paphiopedilum orchids need to be watered more frequently than most epiphytes.

For appropriate aeration, the roots of this orchid should be potted in a bark mix rather than traditional soil. The mix can be of a finer grain than that recommended for vandas, but must still be well-aerated.

Dendrobium

Dendrobiums have thick canes that serve the same purpose as pseudobulbs. They also have velamen roots, and their leaves are stiff and thick.

Orchid canes store food and nutrition and can help an orchid survive a dry season. Like pseudobulbs, canes indicate drought tolerance. The dendrobium's thick leaves have a strong protective cuticle—another sign that this orchid does not need frequent watering.

Aerial velamen roots indicate an epiphytic orchid. It should be potted in a coarse potting mix with excellent drainage to provide the exposure to the air its roots need.

Jewel orchid

Jewel orchids grow under heavy tree canopies and have thick, fleshy stems. One of the most common jewel orchids, *Ludisia discolor*, is native to the South Pacific. Its leaves are thin and flexible and its roots look much like those of familiar houseplants.

L. discolor doesn't have velamen roots and can be grown in a lightweight soilless potting mix like other houseplants. A soil-based mix is not recommended because it would hold too much moisture and could lead to rot.

Jewel orchids tolerate lower light levels than most orchids, making them useful houseplants.

While the thick, fleshy stems of jewel orchids indicate water-storage ability, the thin leaves indicate low drought tolerance. The truth about moisture retention is somewhere in the middle.

Above left: **Paphiopedilums can't store much water, so they need more frequent watering.**

Above center: **Slender canes are typical of dendrobiums.**

Above right: **Jewel orchids don't have velamen roots. Instead, *Ludisia discolor* grows with fleshy stems and dark, flexible leaves.**

choosing the right orchid

As with any garden, choosing the right plant for the right place is crucial. When you understand which orchids grow best in your indoor garden and where you can find them, you're well on your way to success.

p.38
CREATING THE RIGHT GROWING CONDITIONS

Your orchid will thrive when you give it what it needs: the correct light, water, temperature, and growing medium. Each type of orchid has its own requirements.

p.44
CHOOSING ORCHIDS

Fragrance, color, and bloom size and shape are considerations when selecting which orchids to grow. Before you buy, understand the orchids that best suit the growing conditions at your house.

p.50
WHAT SIZE TO PURCHASE

Orchids come in all shapes and sizes. You can start with tiny seedlings that take years to mature but don't cost very much, or you can select a large plant for big bucks.

GROWING CONDITIONS:
Light

The single most important variable when growing orchids is light.

Learning to correctly evaluate your indoor light is of the utmost importance. If you put a full-sun orchid in a low-light location, you're doomed from the get-go. You'll have to decide for yourself whether a tree in front of your west-facing window turns your sill into a medium- or a low-light location.

Of course, nothing is cut and dried. There are orchid types that span the light requirement categories. Some cattleya orchids grow best in high-light conditions while others flourish in medium-high light.

There are several ways to measure light. Every growing situation is unique, but these methods give you someplace to start.

Determining available light

To figure out what kind of light you have, choose a method based on your personality. If you hate technology, use the shadow method. If you're an equipment geek, buy a light meter. Either way, with time you'll develop a feel for light intensity, and ultimately you'll be able to judge with your eye alone.

The shadow method requires nothing fancier than your eyes and one hand. On a sunny day, hold your hand about a foot above the windowsill (or table) where you want to grow an orchid, and look for the shadow cast by your hand. Check the shadow every hour or so. If you can see a dark, sharply outlined shadow for 6 to 8 hours, you have a high-light location.

If you see a shadow with slightly blurred edges, you have a medium-light location. A faint shadow with fuzzy edges indicates low light.

Above: **Phalaenopsis orchids are among the easiest for home gardeners because they need only medium-low light.**

What's a foot-candle?

If you want to be more precise in your measurements, learn about foot-candles. One foot-candle is approximately the amount of light given off by one candle at a distance of one foot.

Orchids can be classified according to the number of foot-candles they need to bloom. High-light orchids need approximately 3,000 foot-candles, medium-light orchids need between 1,500 and 3,000 foot-candles, and low-light orchids need about 1,000 foot-candles.

Orchids are highly adaptable and often pleasantly surprise you by blooming even when light conditions aren't optimal. But why not start off by trying to give each orchid the light it needs?

Using a camera to determine light levels

If you have a single-lens reflex camera, you can use it to measure foot-candles. Set the film speed to ASA 25 and the shutter speed to $\frac{1}{60}$ of a second. Focus on a white sheet of paper in the spot where you want to measure the light and read the f-stop for a correct exposure.

F-STOP	FOOT-CANDLES
2	100
2.8	200
4	370
5.6	750
8	1,500
11	2,800
16	5,000

TEST GARDEN TIP

Get a light meter

If using a camera or the shadow method seems like too much work, or if your inner geek secretly wants to buy another gadget, get yourself a light meter that measures in foot-candles. A decent meter costs $50 to $100 and gives immediate, accurate readings.

The right light
Not every orchid is a tropical sun worshipper. One general rule for most orchids is to avoid direct sunlight. Many prefer bright, indirect light and some want very little light.

HIGH LIGHT
High light means unobstructed sunlight streaming through a clear, south-facing window or into a greenhouse for six to eight hours. High-light orchids include vandas (pictured) and angraecums.

MEDIUM-HIGH LIGHT
Medium-high light describes a location that is quite bright but not necessarily directly sunny. It may receive a combination of direct and indirect light. Eastern and western exposures are often medium-high light locations, although a western exposure may be warmer. As the sun shines throughout the day it warms the air, so afternoon sunshine feels warmer than morning sun. The light intensity is the same, but the air temperature has increased. Oncidiums (pictured), phragmipediums, and dendrobiums grow well in medium-high light locations.

MEDIUM-LOW LIGHT
Medium-low light is appropriate for phalaenopsis (pictured) and paphiopedilum orchids. The best location may be an east- or west-facing window with only indirect light (but no direct sun). It may also be an open northern exposure with no obstructions and some additional reflected light.

LOW LIGHT
Low light is usually found in an area with limited northern exposure or in any exposure where light is blocked by an overhang, trees, or neighboring buildings. Jewel orchids (pictured) can grow in low light.

Location & temperature

Because phalaenopsis orchids need only medium to low light, they do best when direct sunlight is filtered through a curtain.

You can bend the rules a little by rotating your orchids in and out of optimum light.

After all, what's the point of getting that fantastic cattleya to bloom if you can't show it off as a centerpiece for guests? Feel free to bring blooming orchids to a place of prominence in your home, even if there's inadequate light. When the plant finishes flowering, move it back to its growing position.

Measure the temperature

Generally, orchids can be grouped into three temperature categories: cool, warm, and intermediate. Leave a maximum-minimum thermometer (an inexpensive purchase from a hardware or big-box store) in a location for a few days to measure the temperature range. After that, choosing a suitable orchid is simple. As with light, some orchids easily adapt to more than one temperature range.

Cool-growing orchids are native to habitats that, while still tropical, experience colder temperatures than you might expect—it gets cold in the Andes! They thrive in daytime temperatures ranging from 60 to 70°F and nighttime temperatures of 45 to 55°F.

This might seem a little chilly for inside your home, but you'd be surprised at how cool the sill of a bay window gets at night. Perhaps you have a guest room you keep cool when it's not in use, or a large, drafty window; these places would be appropriate for cool-growing orchids.

Warm-growing orchids need daytime temperatures of 80 to 90°F and nighttime temperatures of about 60 to 70°F. It's challenging to grow some of these orchids in the average home, since most of us prefer more moderate temperatures.

Intermediate orchids grow best with daytime temperatures of 70 to 80°F and nighttime temperatures of 55 to 65°F. These are the easiest orchids to grow in most homes.

Grow orchids that suit your lifestyle

In each category, you'll notice there's a difference between daytime and nighttime temperatures. This is something that occurs naturally outdoors, where the sun delivers both light and heat.

Many orchids grow without the temperature differential, but they may not bloom. Take a look at the temperature ranges. If any of them seem like they'd make you uncomfortable, choose your orchids from a category better suited to the way you live.

In winter you can program your thermostat to drop at night; ten degrees' difference would work. In summertime, leave your orchids near open windows where they can take advantage of the natural temperature changes.

TEST GARDEN TIP

Temperature changes help produce blooms

During the warmth of the day, plants manufacture carbohydrates using photosynthesis, then metabolize them for various cellular functions. Cooler nighttime temperatures allow a plant to store the carbohydrates manufactured during the day. That stored nutrition supports flower formation, and without it, orchids may not have enough energy to bloom.

Left: **A maximum-minimum thermometer that also shows relative humidity is a useful tool in managing your orchids.**

Above: **Phalaenopsis and dendrobium orchids love spending summers outdoors where they can get bright light, but not direct sun.**

Humidity

To round out the big three conditions of orchid growing,

consider humidity. Most orchids grown as houseplants come from the tropics, and most parts of the tropics are much more humid than the average living room.

That's a good thing as far as mildewed carpet and warped bookshelves are concerned, but your orchids—in fact, most of your houseplants—will grow better if you boost the humidity in their immediate growing area.

Check the humidity

Obviously, humidity levels vary greatly depending on your location (Santa Fe, for example, differs from Baltimore) and the season. You can buy an inexpensive humidity gauge (humidistat) at your favorite hardware store, or consider a a combination humidistat/minimum-maximum thermometer.

Place the gauge on your windowsill and check it in an hour or two. In a climate-controlled home

Above: **For humidity without overwatering, place orchids on a bed of pebbles that are nearly covered with water. Be sure the roots are not sitting in the water.**

Opposite: **Elevate your orchids on egg-crate louvers, a plastic lattice used to diffuse light, available in large sheets at hardware or big-box stores. For extra humidity, add water to just below the plants.**

environment, an average windowsill probably offers 15 to 20 percent humidity.

In contrast, a tropical rain forest averages 75 to 90 percent humidity. You'll never reach that level of humidity indoors, nor do you need to, but it's a good idea to raise the humidity in your orchid growing area if possible.

Humidity changes by season

Winter humidity levels can be as low as 10 to 15 percent. If you've ever awakened on a January morning with a dry nose and parched throat, you know this.

The amount of moisture air can hold is directly related to temperature. Cold air holds less moisture than warm air before reaching the dew point. That's the point at which moisture condenses out of the air in the form of water. Air at 50°F with relative humidity of 30 percent holds less moisture than air at 70°F with the same relative humidity.

In winter, the relative humidity in a home drops. Cold air is drier than warm air and can't hold as much water vapor.

As the air inside the home is heated, it becomes capable of holding more moisture but the relative humidity decreases unless moisture is added at the same time.

Avoid spritzing

Put down the spray bottle! Spritzing your orchids is less helpful than you might think. As soon as the water has evaporated (which is pretty quickly), you'll need to spray again. Unless you plan to quit your job to stay home and spritz your plants, there are better solutions.

The easiest thing to do is to group your plants together. Water is a byproduct of photosynthesis and is given off as vapor through openings in the plants' leaves, called stomata. This process is transpiration. Transpiration raises the humidity of the air immediately surrounding your plants. So, grouping your plants together can increase local humidity.

Take a humidity reading with an inexpensive gauge next to a single orchid. Then group five or six orchids together, wait 10 to 12 hours, and take another reading from the center of the group. It should be higher by as much as 10 percent.

Other humidity solutions

Another easy fix is to create a dry well. Add a ½- to 1-inch layer of pebbles to your orchids' existing watertight saucers or to a baking sheet for a group of orchids. Place the orchids on top of the pebbles and pour water onto the pebbles to just below the bottom of the pots.

As the water evaporates from around the pebbles, it raises the ambient humidity. Since the pots aren't sitting in water, the orchids' roots won't stay dangerously wet.

A slightly more sophisticated method is to use plastic egg-crate louvers, a specialty item originally designed as diffusers for light fixtures. The plastic can be cut to fit inside any tray, where it supports orchid pots above the evaporating water. You can also purchase orchid trays fitted with ready-made racks.

If you're growing mounted orchids, which don't sit on trays, or if you simply want to go all out, consider a humidifier. Beware: If you have hard water, ultrasonic (mist) humidifiers can leave a residue of mineral deposits on orchid leaves. It won't hurt your plants, but it doesn't look pretty.

An evaporative humidifier won't create this problem. With its built-in humidistat, the machine kicks in only when humidity dips below a programmed level.

TEST GARDEN TIP

Spend summers outside

If you have space outdoors, give your plants a summer vacation. Protect them from the sun; in unobstructed sunlight, even sun-loving orchids get leaf burn. Dappled light under a trellis is perfect. You can also hang orchid pots from the branches of a leafy tree. Rain cuts your watering chores.

Choosing orchids

Consider color and fragrance when selecting an orchid. If you're decorating with an orchid, you can just slip the existing pot into a decorative cachepot.

What are you looking for in an orchid?

Are you seduced by exotic perfume, or do you swoon at the sight of a deep-purple flower? To select your ideal orchid, focus on the characteristics most important to you.

Many orchids are fragrant

Fragrance is completely subjective; one person's preferred perfume is another's fish head. It's worth sniffing a few flowers to decide if you like the scent before choosing a plant for your home. Although some orchids have no scent, here are a few that are known for their fragrance.

The smell of *Oncidium* Sharry Baby has been described as either vanilla or chocolate.

Brassavola nodosa has a classic sweet perfume akin to lily-of-the-valley and is most fragrant at night.

Miniature *Haraella retrocalla odorata* (sometimes sold as *H. odorata*) blooms several times a year. Its yellow flowers carry the scent of citrus.

The fragrance of *Cochleanthes amazonica* may remind you of candy, while that of *Cattleya walkeriana* is reminiscent of vanilla.

The common name for *Maxillariella tenuifolia* is the coconut orchid—that's what it smells like.

Oncidium Twinkle 'Fragrance Fantasy' is a white-flowered miniature orchid with a sweet scent. O. Twinkle 'Red Fantasy' has a similar perfume.

Consider color and bloom size

For those who avoid floral perfume, there are plenty of orchids with no scent. In this case, it's all about the visual.

There's no denying orchids are beautiful to look at. They come in almost every color, from serene pastels to powerful, saturated hues. Flowers may be monochromatic or combine several colors in a single bloom.

There are striped and spotted orchids, orchids with lips that contrast with their petals, even orchids whose flowers look like the insects they're trying to attract.

Once you've chosen a color palette and pattern, think about bloom size. Would you rather have a single giant flower or numerous small blooms?

Finally, consider length of the bloom period. Phalaenopsis orchids are well-known for their long bloom life. It's not unusual for their flowers to persist for several months.

Left: **Sharry Baby oncidium carries a delightful scent that can be described as either chocolate or vanilla.**

Above: **Boost the cheeriness factor in any room by grouping brightly colored orchids.**

Which orchid to buy?

Of course you can buy orchids at a florist or a plant nursery, but you can also find them online, in big-box stores, and even at grocery stores.

It's possible to find healthy, quality orchids in all these places if you know what to look for. Take a few minutes to inspect your prospective purchase and ask yourself these questions:

Is the foliage a healthy light green? If it's an odd color, check to ensure that is normal for this orchid.

Are the flower buds plump? Avoid shriveled buds.

Is the plant insect-free? Inspect the pot and roots carefully.

Does the potting mix smell good? Take a sniff: wet, rotting roots emit a distinctive odor that can help you avoid a mistake.

Above: **An orchid in bloom is an enticing sight. Before you buy, check for healthy foliage and roots and plump flower buds. Inspect for pests and sniff the potting medium; avoid buying it if the mix doesn't smell fresh.**

Watch for bud blast

Bud blast is the term used when orchid buds look shriveled or yellow. It's a sure sign that something went very wrong. Look for it before you buy.

Bud blast can be caused by several things, but the most common causes are over- or underwatering, and overly hot or cold temperatures at a crucial stage in flowering.

Blasted buds never open; they just fall off and break your heart. Sometimes the problem occurs when the plants are in transit, and sometimes bud blast happens because the store put the orchid display too close to an outside door.

If you see an orchid display close to an outside door, check the plants carefully before buying. The good news is that it takes colder temperatures to kill a plant than it does to blast a bud. So even though it gets cold enough to shrivel the flower buds, the plant may live to bloom again.

ASK THE GARDEN DOCTOR

How do I grow an unidentified orchid?

ANSWER: If an orchid with no identification has variegated leaves, give it bright indirect light but no direct sun. If it has large pseudobulbs, let it dry out between waterings. If it has pale green foliage, give it high light. If the leaves are thin, water every three to five days. You can learn a lot by trial and error.

Left: **The shriveled bud on this phalaenopsis orchid succumbed to bud blast. It can be caused by a variety of actions, including over- or underwatering or exposure to too much heat or cold.**

Below: **When buying an orchid, pay attention to the foliage. Do you prefer long, straplike leaves, or are rounded leaves more to your liking? Remember that the orchid won't be in bloom all of the time, so choose a pleasing foliage form.**

Orchid buying considerations

A paphiopedilum in full bloom emerges from shipping in perfect condition when packed by an experienced orchid supplier.

Sometimes, if an orchid has finished flowering

or it has a few brown leaves, you can strike a bargain with the seller, even at national retail chains. As long as you confirm that the plant is basically healthy, it's worth a try.

While beginning growers may prefer to start with perfect, blooming orchids, those with more experience know how to clean up an unkempt plant. It's not easy for the store to sell a tired-looking orchid; you may be able to get two for the price of one.

Need customer service?

If you need old-fashioned customer service, you're better off shopping with a florist or at a traditional garden center where the staff should know something about what they're selling.

If you're comfortable making an unassisted purchase, grocery stores and megavendors can offer great deals. With time and experience, you'll be able to make decisions on your own.

Shopping on the Internet

Online vendors have much bigger selections of plants than most stores, and it's often less expensive to buy directly from a grower located where the climate makes orchid cultivation less expensive. After all, where do you think it costs more to grow an orchid, Hawaii or Massachusetts?

Remember that shipping an orchid is a delicate task. Orchids are fragile, especially when they're in bud or bloom. They're susceptible to damage from cold as well as breakage and must be exceptionally well-packaged to arrive intact. Many commercial orchid growers won't ship during winter because it's not worth the risk posed by an unheated cargo bay.

Protect your purchase

If you're carrying an orchid home when the weather outside is frightful, there are a few things you can do to protect your purchase.

Place it gently inside a picnic-style cooler bag. Or if you have only a short distance to travel, wrap the plant in a paper sleeve or plastic bag and button it inside your coat, where your body heat will keep it warm.

TEST GARDEN TIP

Grow your own orchids to nibble

If you get an orchid flower as garnish in a restaurant, don't assume it's edible. Flowers are often used to decorate a plate, but if they've been sprayed for pests and diseases, they could be toxic. A homegrown dendrobium flower is safe to eat, but unless you're sure a plant has been raised organically it's better not to nibble.

Left: **Ordering orchids online is useful for home growers who want a larger selection.**

What size to purchase

The cliché is true: You get what you pay for.
There are benefits to buying orchids at either end of the size and quality spectrum, whether you spend $5 for a bare-root seedling or $55 for a mature plant in bloom.

Pros and cons of larger or smaller plants
Beginning growers are often better off with mature plants. The immediate gratification of gorgeous blooms boosts morale, plus you start out with a plant that is strong and well-grown. An orchid in full regalia is hard to resist. Yes, you pay a little more, but you're guaranteed a successful flower, which can give you enough confidence to try another.

Above: **Mature orchids produce bigger, stronger blooms.**

Plants in bud may be slightly less expensive, but the bud stage is sensitive and susceptible to damage. On the other hand, plants in bud are smaller and easier to ship or transport than orchids with fully opened flowers. Both flowering orchids and plants in bud are sometimes labeled blooming-size plants.

Young plants cost less, but you may have to wait months or years for them to bloom. If you're a patient gardener, or you have other orchids to keep you occupied, buying inexpensive young plants is an excellent way to build a collection.

If the young orchid is a named cultivar purchased from a reputable grower, you can be sure you'll get what you paid for. If the plant has no label, you'll have to wait for the flower to see what you have.

How to grow seedlings

Seedlings are the least expensive plants to buy, and they take the most work to grow. You can purchase a flask of seedlings directly from a commercial grower, but deflasking and growing such young plants is an ambitious project for the beginner.

During their transition from seedling to young plant, seedlings are especially susceptible to pests and diseases.

Small or bare-root orchids are sometimes sold as seedlings, although they are simply young plants. These orchids have already made the leap from the rarified atmosphere of the laboratory flask to open-air growing in bark media, which is key.

They may require more frequent attention than a mature plant while their root systems develop and they adjust to the humidity and light of a home growing situation. When you've bloomed your first orchid grown from a young bare-root plant, you'll feel a great sense of accomplishment.

ASK THE GARDEN DOCTOR

How tough are seedlings?

ANSWER: Seedlings are delicate. They have fewer roots and more tender tissue than mature specimens of the same species. Pay close attention to their needs and provide more frequent watering and lower light levels than for established plants.

Above: **Three sizes of cattleyas for sale show the difference between a small plant and a large, blooming one.**

Right: **When purchasing a bare-root orchid, you can note the health of the roots and choose your own potting medium.**

how to grow

Should you grow your orchid in sun or shade? Pot it in fine- or coarse-grain mix? Plant it in a clay, plastic, or slatted wood container? For each type of orchid, you'll make a separate choice.

p.54
ANALYZING GROWING CONDITIONS

Many orchids require different growing conditions than typical houseplants. Check your environment to be sure it provides the kind of light and humidity your orchid prefers.

p.58
CHOOSING THE RIGHT POTTING MIX

Stay away from potting soil when it comes to growing orchids. Special mixes ensure each type of root gets the air and moisture it needs.

p.60
SELECTING CONTAINERS

Each orchid grows best with a certain type of pot. Check this section to see whether plastic, clay, a slatted wood basket, or a slab of bark is best.

Analyzing your growing conditions

In nature, many orchids grow on trees. If you live in a tropical climate, you can grow orchids outdoors year-round.

Growing conditions differ from location to location.

For example, if you live in Hawaii, southern Florida, or southern California, you may be able to grow orchids outdoors year-round. In other places, you can grow orchids using a combination of indoors and out. But geographic location isn't only important because of temperature. It also influences humidity and light levels.

Where temperatures stay reliably warm, go ahead and hang vandas from the palm trees in your yard, then kick back. Outdoor growing in tropical or subtropical locales means you can take advantage of naturally high humidity, bright light, obliging rains, and warm temperatures.

Where you live matters

Humidity can be high in the Pacific Northwest, but light levels are lower because the greater distance from the equator translates to a lower angle of the sun and also because tree cover may be heavier. Temperatures there are moderate year round, so while you could summer your orchids outdoors in some areas, warm-growing orchids won't flourish.

In the desert Southwest there's an entirely different combination of circumstances: high summer temperatures and intense light, but woefully low humidity. To grow orchids there you'll need a swamp cooler or humidifier running most of the time.

What about urban orchid growers? Surrounding buildings may block a significant amount of light to apartment windows on low floors. If you're lucky enough to have a terrace, you could hang your orchids outdoors in warm weather, but city soot should be cleaned off when you bring your plants inside.

Left: **Blooming orchids make beautiful home decorations. When the flowers are done, move the plant into the proper light conditions. For specifics, see the Gallery of Orchids on page 130.**

Above: **It's fine to keep a phalaenopsis orchid near a sunny window, but protect it from direct exposure, especially during the summer.**

Orchids need a special climate

Many gardeners take climate control for granted. They turn on the air-conditioner in the summer and the heat in the winter, keeping their homes between 65 and 75°F.

This means that they can grow orchids across a wide range of outdoor climate zones, with a few exceptions. Intermediate-temperature orchids are generally happy wherever people are comfortable.

But others require more sacrifice if you want to grow them indoors. Be prepared to turn off the air-conditioning if you want warm-growers or to lower the heat for cool-growing orchids.

The best orchid home: a greenhouse

The ultimate goal of any serious orchid grower is a greenhouse. There, you can capture maximum sunshine, create areas of shade when needed, add humidity, regulate heat, and automate irrigation.

Above: **Cattleyas can be placed in dappled sunlight or bright shade outdoors or near a sunny window indoors.**

No matter what part of the country you live in, inside the greenhouse it's paradise. Most people aren't that lucky, and truth is, you don't need a greenhouse to grow beautiful orchids. But it is nice to dream.

Keep orchids out of full outdoor sun

Any orchid you move outdoors into the sun needs protection. Indoor orchids in a south-facing window get less than half the light that they would outdoors because plain glass filters out more than half of the sun's intensity.

Place your plants in full shade for several days while they get acclimated to being outdoors. Some, such as phalaenopsis and paphiopedilums, should stay in the shade.

Others, such as dendrobiums, cattleyas, and cymbidiums, can be placed in dappled sunlight or bright shade after a few days. (Bright shade is shade well illuminated by reflected light.)

Lovers of high light, such as vandas, angraecums, and brassavolas, can eventually be moved into dappled light, but they will suffer sunburn without some shelter. Don't worry if you see some red pigment on the foliage. Some orchids produce this in response to high light. It doesn't harm the plant and should revert to green when lower light levels are achieved.

However, if you notice brown, burned splotches on your orchid's foliage, move the plant to a more protected position.

Protect from below-50 temperatures

At the end of summer, before temperatures dip into the 50s, move your orchids back indoors. Cymbidiums can stay outside until the mercury drops into the 40s—indeed, this temperature drop in fall is essential for cymbidiums to set buds.

Check all your orchids for insect pests before bringing them inside. Check especially for slugs. They may hitchhike indoors hidden in the bark mix.

TEST
GARDEN
TIP

Orchid temperature ranges

Many tropical orchids are surprisingly tough and can tolerate temperatures in the 40s and 50s when they're not in bloom. A few, especially those that originate in higher elevations in nature, can survive an occasional dip below freezing. Super-hot temperatures can be as dangerous as super-cold ones. Even warm-growing orchids can suffer from heat stress. Overheating can suppress bloom, cause bud blast, burn foliage, and generally weaken a plant. Aim to keep even your heat-loving orchids cooler than 85°F.

Left: **High-light orchids appreciate being lifted closer to the light source, although they can burn if left in continuous bright sun outdoors.**

Above: **Orchid leaves, such as the one on this dendrobium, turn brown and crisp when sunburned.**

Choosing the right potting mix

Sphagnum moss is often used as a potting mix because it retains moisture. But because the moss can look dry when it's actually wet, it's easy to overwater and kill an orchid.

You may have noticed that most orchids grown as houseplants aren't potted in traditional potting mix. Jewel orchids can be potted in a traditional soilless potting mix, but that's as far as it goes.

Some orchids aren't even grown in traditional pots. Because most of them are epiphytes, their roots would quickly rot if surrounded by soil or even a soilless mix.

So what should you use instead, and once you figure that out, what container should you put the plant in? The choice depends on which plants you grow, and to a lesser extent, how much work you want to put into the growing.

Choose specialized bark mixes

You already know that orchid roots are special. Aerial roots require excellent contact with the air, which is why they are grown in bark mix instead of potting soil.

Epiphytes and lithophytes can be potted in a medium- to coarse-grain bark mix. In nature, these orchids dry out between frequent rains, and you can mimic these conditions by providing them with a bark mix that allows the roots to dry between waterings.

Orchids that grow better with more-consistent moisture (such as phragmipediums, paphiopedilums, and miltonias) can be potted in a fine-grain mix. The bark pieces are smaller, which means they provide more surface area and hold more moisture.

The perils of sphagnum moss

One of the most common potting materials used for orchids is long-grain sphagnum moss. Commercial growers use the soft, pliable fiber for several reasons. First, it retains moisture for a long time, which means less watering. Second, it stays in the pot when orchids are in transit.

If an orchid potted in bark mix tips over, the bark mix spills and the orchid may come out of the pot. If you tip over an orchid potted in long-grain sphagnum moss, nothing is lost.

But there's a downside. If you buy an orchid potted in sphagnum, you should repot it in bark mix as soon as the orchid finishes blooming.

Here's why: Sphagnum moss is difficult for beginning growers to use. The surface of the moss feels dry to the touch several days after watering, but the moss inside the pot surrounding the orchid's roots can still be moist 7 to 10 days later.

It's far too easy to overwater an orchid that is planted in sphagnum moss. Many a good orchid has been lost as a result.

Growing in rocks

You may find the most drought-tolerant epiphytes and lithophytes sold potted in what looks like rocks. This could be gravel, lava rock, or expanded ceramic pellets.

All of these drain well, but because they are inorganic, they provide no nutrition to the orchids. Orchids will need more-frequent fertilization than those planted in bark mixes.

ASK THE GARDEN DOCTOR

Can I use potting soil?

ANSWER: No. Tropical orchids should be grown in a special mix that provides their roots access to air. Potting soil is too heavy and retains moisture too long to sustain healthy root growth.

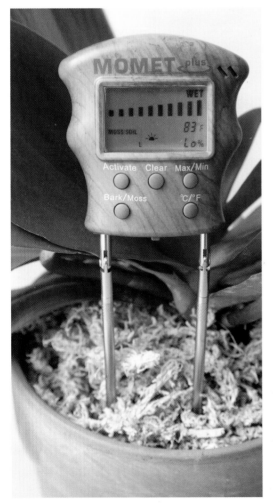

Left: **You can tuck your finger into potting mix up to the first knuckle to feel for moisture, or use a meter that is calibrated to read moisture in either bark or moss mixes.**

Above: **Orchids that need more moisture, including slipper orchids, prefer a fine bark mix, shown on left, while other orchids like the extra air spaces provided by a coarse mix, right.**

Selecting containers

Not only do orchids require specialized potting mixes, but many also benefit from specialized containers. Orchid pots have additional holes and slits in their sides and bottoms to improve drainage and aeration.

Materials for pots range from plain black plastic to unglazed terra-cotta or artistic glazed clay. Many orchids grow perfectly well in traditional pots, but if the idea of specialized gear appeals to you, or if you have an inclination to overwater, try a container with built-in aeration.

Clay or plastic pots?

Unglazed clay is porous. Water evaporates through the walls of a clay pot, making it an excellent vessel for orchids because they like to dry out between waterings. If you live someplace with high humidity or if you grow in a greenhouse, clay is a good choice. A clay pot can also help balance a tendency to overwater.

Plastic is nonporous, meaning no water evaporates from the potting mix through the walls of the pot. This ensures that the mix and the roots in a plastic container stay moist longer than they would in a clay pot.

Above: **A complete orchid potting bench includes a variety of containers to have on hand, from slatted boxes for drought-tolerant orchids to plastic containers for moisture-loving ones. Phragmepediums, for example, are high-light, moisture-loving orchids that grow best in plastic.**

Terrestrial orchids, such as paphiopedilums and phragmipediums, prefer more moisture than epiphytes and can be grown in plastic.

If you forget to water plants or have time to only water once a week, growing your orchids in plastic buys you an extra day or two between waterings. On the other hand, just because an orchid comes potted in plastic doesn't mean it should stay that way. Commercial growers use plastic pots because they're less likely to break in transit, less expensive to manufacture, and lighter weight so they're easier and less expensive to ship.

Wooden and woven containers

Some drought-tolerant orchids grow best with more root exposure to air than any pot can provide. You'll often see vandas, encyclias, and angraecums sold in slatted wooden baskets or woven plastic containers. These orchids can be grown with little or no bark mix or with their roots wrapped in moss. Mounted orchids—plants attached to a chunk of cork, wood, or fern fiber—may be held in place using only their aerial roots.

Orchids without pots

Mounted orchids and orchids perched in baskets without potting media require higher humidity and more frequent watering than orchids grown in pots. If you live someplace tropical, or if you have a greenhouse, your humidity may be high enough to grow bark-mounted orchids. In the average home, these grow best in the presence of a humidifier or with frequent dunks in the tub or sink. This could be once a day or every other day, depending how dry the air is. A sunny bathroom is a great spot for a mounted orchid, where the mist from a daily shower humidifies the air.

TEST GARDEN TIP

Wait to repot

Depending on your skill, repotting can be traumatic to an orchid, causing it to drop its flowers and buds. Always wait to repot until the plant has finished blooming.

Below left: **Vanda orchids, usually potted in a slatted wood box or woven container, like high humidity and high light.**

Below right: **You can dress up a potted orchid by placing it inside a cachepot, a decorative vessel with no drainage holes. Just don't allow the orchid to remain in standing water.**

care &
maintenance

Orchids are special plants that need special care. Growing them is no more difficult than growing other plants—it's just a little different.

p.64
WATERING

Because orchids grow in a bark potting medium—or even right on top of a piece of bark—they need to be watered differently than other houseplants.

p.68
FERTILIZING

Many orchids grow well without fertilizer—just as they do in nature—but the frequency, size, and number of blooms can be boosted with fertilizer.

p.72
GROOMING

Just like people, orchids benefit from a bit of grooming now and then. It's easy to keep leaves and flowers looking tip-top.

p.82
DIVIDING & REPOTTING

Dividing and repotting an orchid that has grown too big for its pot or is suffering from old potting medium is almost as easy as repotting any other plant.

Watering

Soaking a clay pot in a sink or bowl of water hydrates both the pot and the bark mix.

If you have ever watered an orchid

you know that most of what you pour in runs out almost immediately through the bottom of the pot.

Because orchids are grown in bark mix rather than potting soil, they need to be watered differently. When you water a plant in soil, the water that fills the air spaces between soil particles is held in place by a combination of adhesive force and surface tension.

However, because the spaces between pieces of bark mix are much larger, adhesion and surface tension cannot hold the water in place for longer than a few seconds.

The goal in watering orchids is not to fill the spaces between the mix particles with water. Instead, each particle should absorb as much water as possible through its surfaces.

Watering clay pots or slabs

To get the most benefit from each watering, the bark pieces in clay pots should be soaked. Pouring water into the pot (and having it run out again five seconds later) barely moistens the mix.

To give the mix time to absorb enough water, place the entire pot in a bowl of water for 10 to 15 minutes, then lift it out and let the excess water drain before returning the pot back to its usual location.

Since clay pots are porous, water also penetrates the walls of the pot at the same time it's absorbed by the bark, adding to the moisture reserves available to the orchid.

You can water orchids mounted on bark or fiber slabs the same way.

Watering orchids in plastic pots

Since water can't pass through plastic, place the potted orchid in an empty bowl, then add water.

Add the water to just below the lip of the pot and let it sit for 10 to 15 minutes, then drain and put the pot back in place.

If you place the plastic pot in an already-full bowl of water, the water will push the bark up and out, floating it away from the orchid's roots.

Watering orchids in sphagnum

If you're growing an orchid potted in long-grain sphagnum moss or soilless mix, you can water it like a regular potted plant, until water runs out into the saucer below.

But remember, sphagnum moss may feel dry on its surface while the interior is still moist. Stick your finger an inch or two down into the moss to feel whether it's truly dry.

TEST GARDEN TIP

Retain moisture

Clay pots and wooden orchid boxes are porous and can rob moisture from potting mix, causing your orchid's roots to dry out. Soaking the porous container allows the potting mix to stay moist longer, whether it's bark mix, sphagnum moss, or soilless potting mix.

Left: **Water poured over a bark mix immediately runs out the bottom and doesn't give the mix enough time to absorb moisture.**

Above: **Fill a sink or tub large enough to hold a bark slab with water. Because the bark floats, you may need to hold or weigh it down.**

Use a turkey baster to remove excess water from an orchid container drywell.

Your watering schedule will be different for different kinds of orchids.

A good general rule is to plan on watering once a week for drought-tolerant orchids (cattleyas, oncidiums, dendrobiums), and once every four to five days for others (miltonias, paphiopedilums, phragmipediums).

Start with those guidelines, and adjust up or down according to the conditions in your home.

For example, if you have a moderately drought-tolerant orchid like a phalaenopsis potted in sphagnum moss in a plastic pot, you may only need to water it every 10 days because both the sphagnum and plastic conserve water.

The same orchid potted in bark in a clay pot might need water every seven days. Stick your fingers down into the potting mix to feel for moisture. Drought-tolerant orchids should be allowed to dry out thoroughly between waterings.

If you feel any moisture with your fingers, wait a day, then test again. To be sure, use a moisture meter especially made for orchids.

Specific orchids need special watering

Specific recommendations for watering different species may be found in the Gallery of Orchids on page 130. Remember that what changes from plant to plant is the frequency of your watering, not the amount of water delivered.

All orchids should be thoroughly moistened each time, then allowed to dry out before you water them again.

TEST GARDEN TIP

Don't bother to mist

Hand-misting is a waste of time. Keep plants on a drywell or a tray suspended over water to increase ambient humidity. Mounted orchids can be misted more effectively and efficiently with a humidifier than by hand.

Watering tips
How frequently you water your orchid can depend on many things. Answer these questions before you pour:

What kind of orchid are you growing—drought-resistant or not? Drought-resistant plants need water less frequently.

What kind of pot is it in? Porous pots such as clay dry out faster than nonporous pots such as plastic.

What kind of potting mix is it in? Sphagnum moss needs water less frequently than bark mix.

How warm is your home? Plants dry out faster in warmer temperatures.

How humid is the air? Plants stay moister in humid air.

How much light does your orchid get? Plants growing in brighter light need more water.

Fertilizing

Fertilize phalaenopsis orchids as usual until they finish blooming, then withhold fertilizer for a month or two.

Potted plants get their nutrition from three sources:
sunlight, potting mix, and fertilizer.

Potting mix delivers nutrients to plants via biodegradation. As it breaks down, the mix makes nutrients available to plant roots. However, consider how coarse bark is compared to traditional potting soil. A coarse mix biodegrades much more slowly than a fine mix, so it releases fewer nutrients. Bark-mounted orchids get even less nutrition since they are not potted in mix.

Many orchids need no fertilizer
Fortunately, most orchids are not heavy feeders. Many orchids bloom year after year with no fertilizer at all.

During active growth, when new leaves are being produced, you may fertilize every other time you water, using half the strength recommended on the fertilizer package. You may have heard the phrase "fertilize weakly, weekly." This summarizes the philosophy of delivering a small amount of nutrition with each watering.

It's important to deliver plain water without fertilizer at least once a month to flush excess salts from the bark mix and avoid fertilizer burn to the roots.

Winter fertilizing varies
Many orchids are inactive in winter and don't need fertilizer. Others, notably phalaenopsis and cymbidium orchids, bloom during the winter months. These should be fed as usual until they finish blooming. Then give them a break of one to two months without fertilizer. As days lengthen and temperatures increase, watch for new growth and begin fertilizing again.

TEST GARDEN TIP

Fertilizer optional

Many orchids bloom without ever needing fertilizer. But if you do decide to feed your orchids, remember the adage to "fertilize weakly, weekly."

Fertilizing orchids Liquid fertilizers are the best options for orchids. There are two main delivery methods: soaking the growing medium and feeding the leaves.

TAKE A DIP Soak orchids in a liquid fertilizer solution so the bark mix absorbs nutrients along with water. Mix the fertilizer according to package directions so you don't overfertilize the orchid.

GIVE IT A SPRITZ You can fertilize with a foliar feed. Add the fertilizer (mixed to the proper formulation) to a spray bottle and spray it onto the foliage and velamen roots, where it can be absorbed.

Analyzing fertilizer

Orchids, such as this phalaenopsis, may benefit from a bloom booster (fertilizer with extra phosphorus) to form large, vigorous blooms.

Most orchids grow well with balanced fertilizers.

These contain equal amounts of nitrogen, phosphates, and potassium to encourage strong all-around growth.

A balanced fertilizer should be marked with three equal numbers, such as 5-5-5 or 10-10-10, indicating the percentage of the fertilizer by weight of each nutritional component. These numbers are called the guaranteed analysis.

Nitrogen promotes healthy, green foliage; phosphates provide phosphorus to support flower production; and potassium assists with root development and disease resistance.

Check the nitrogen

Take a look at the label on the fertilizer and check the nitrogen analysis. You may see nitrogen broken down into one or more of the following categories: nitrate nitrogen, ammoniacal nitrogen, and urea nitrogen.

Urea is not a useful source of nitrogen for orchids potted in bark mix. In soil, naturally occurring bacteria break down urea, making it available to plant roots. But since most orchids are potted in bark, and because the bacteria do not live in bark, the urea in the fertilizer breaks down slowly. It is flushed out of the bark mix long before it can be absorbed, essentially wasted. To get your money's worth, choose a fertilizer without urea.

No extra nitrogen needed

For years it was assumed that bark-grown orchids (mounted or potted) needed extra nitrogen. The fungi that break down wood also consume large amounts of nitrogen, and botanists thought growers should make up for this consumption by adding extra nitrogen to the potting mix. High-nitrogen fertilizers had formulas like 30-10-10.

Now, however, this is no longer recommended. It's believed excess nitrogen promotes foliage growth at the expense of flowers.

What's a bloom booster?

A bloom booster is a fertilizer with a higher percentage of phosphates, indicated by a formula with a higher middle number, like 10-60-10.

While the number-one reason for lack of bloom is insufficient light, nutrition can be a contributing factor.

You may see fertilizers labeled as orchid food or African violet food on the shelf. If so, check the guaranteed analysis. They are basically bloom-booster fertilizers and are appropriate for use with any flowering plant.

Why to stay balanced

You can find recommendations for high-nitrogen and bloom-booster fertilizers, but most likely neither is necessary. The high phosphorus of a bloom booster may be needed only to balance a fertilizer with extra nitrogen that promotes foliage growth over flowers.

Stick with a balanced fertilizer unless you see signs of a specific nutritional deficiency.

Fertilizer to avoid

Several forms of fertilizers do not work well for orchids. Granular plant food and fertilizer sticks are both basically useless.

In traditional potting mix, fertilizer sticks are gradually broken down by soil moisture. Nutrients are transported out and away from the stick by water, moving throughout the volume of soil in the pot.

In bark mix, a fertilizer stick can't dissolve in the same way because parts of the stick make no contact with bark mix. Nor are the nutrients distributed evenly throughout the pot because water travels less uniformly through bark mix than it does through potting soil.

Granular fertilizer is also dissolved by moisture, a process that requires time. When used in conjunction with bark mix, many of the granules simply wash out of the mix before they have a chance to dissolve.

ASK THE GARDEN DOCTOR

Why isn't my orchid blooming?

ANSWER: Lack of sufficient light and insufficient night-time temperature drops are the two top reasons for lack of blooms, but nutrition can be a contributing factor. In the Gallery of Orchids, starting on page 130, check the requirements for your type of orchid to find what it's missing.

Above: **Look for a fertilizer without urea, a form of nitrogen that orchids can't use. The relatively high middle number on this label indicates a high phosphorus content, which will help promote flowering.**

Right: **The best types of orchid fertilizers are liquids or fine-grain powders (to be diluted with water), shown in the two bowls in front. Sticks and coated granules, shown in the two back bowls, don't perform well in orchid bark mix.**

Good grooming

This oncidium is perfectly groomed: The leaves are dusted, unsightly leaves have been removed, and the tall bloom spikes are staked to display the "dancing ladies" flowers.

A little care and attention to an orchid's appearance work wonders.

Maintaining leaves, roots, and flowers keeps your plants healthy and looking their best. You need a few ordinary household tools: A pair of scissors, pruners, a pair of cotton socks, a feather duster, dishwashing liquid, twist ties, and stakes will get you started.

One of the easiest things you can do is dust your orchid. Dust and soot can clog leaf pores, decreasing the efficiency of photosynthesis and reducing the amount of nutrition available to the plant. A feather duster can remove a light coating of dust from the leaves.

If a thick layer of gummy soot has accumulated, you may need something stronger than a feather duster. Try putting one sock on each hand and gently rubbing the grime from both sides of the leaves.

An orchid on a city windowsill may get so dirty that even the sock treatment is not enough. In this case, take your orchid to the sink and squeeze a little dishwashing liquid onto your fingertips. Rub it onto the foliage (both sides), dissolving the sooty buildup.

Be sure to thoroughly rinse the soap off the leaves. Fertilizer residue can be removed in the same way.

Above: **Keep grooming tools on hand, including mild dish soap, scissors or floral snips, stakes and clips, a soft sock, and a duster. Dust your orchid's leaves before washing them. Otherwise, you might smear dirt into a wet coating of grime.**

What to do about mushy pseudobulbs

As pseudobulbs age they lose their leaves and no longer produce flower spikes. As long as these bulbs remain green and hard they serve a purpose, storing water and nutrition for the plant. If, however, a pseudobulb begins to turn yellow and feel soft or mushy, it's time to remove it. Using sterilized pruners, cut the connecting rhizome between the rotting pseudobulb and the closest healthy pseudobulb. Confirm that the remaining growth is healthy and green throughout, then dust the cut with ground cinnamon (a natural fungicide). For more about orchid surgery, see Chapter 6. When decay sets in, move swiftly to remove the rot before it spreads.

Caring for leaves

Most phalaenopsis
orchids grow
with naturally
shiny leaves.

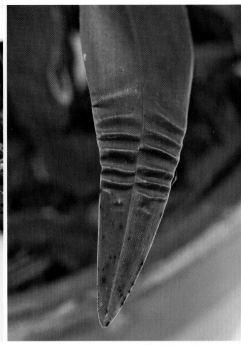

Brown leaves and shriveled pseudobulbs

could be an indication of poor health, but often are signs of neglect. Orchid leaves may turn brown or yellow for many reasons: old age, extreme temperatures, irregular watering, or physical damage. Once the cause of the damage has been determined, correct the problem and remove the evidence.

Cutting leaves

When you cut into plant tissue, make sure you use sterile instruments. If you prune a diseased orchid and then work on a healthy orchid without sterilizing your tools, you could pass the disease from one plant to the next.

To clean the blade, wipe it with rubbing alcohol or a 10 percent bleach solution. Or hold the blade of your cutting tool over a flame (from a lighter or propane torch) for a few seconds. If you choose the flame method, be sure to let the blade cool before using it.

Leaf damage

The leaves at the bottom of a monopodial orchid or the outside of a sympodial plant are the oldest. It's normal for these leaves to fade to yellow or brown and drop off over time.

When the foliage is no longer green, remove it by trimming the leaf back to its point of origin: the top of the pseudobulb, the cane, or the stem. After several years, if you have a large section of stem on a monopodial orchid or many pseudobulbs without foliage on a sympodial orchid, it may be time to divide or repot (see the instructions that begin on page 82).

Damaged leaves will never become whole again. Brown leaf margins (due to over- or underwatering), burned spots (contact with a cold or hot windowpane), and pleated foliage (dehydration) should be removed from the plant, and the remaining portion of the leaf should be trimmed to imitate the original shape of the leaf.

How to keep leaves shiny

Some florists and nurseries spray an oil-based product on plants to make the leaves look shiny and clean. If you like the artificial look of intensely glossy foliage and you use a leaf-shine product, please use it in moderation.

Whether or not the oil-based sprays clog stomata (and the debate over this rages on), the spray can disfigure the leaves it's intended to beautify. If applied unevenly, it can accumulate in sticky blotches that attract dust and grime to the leaf's surface. Some shine products contain minerals that build up over time and are difficult or impossible to remove from the leaf's surface.

There are many recipes for homemade leaf-shine products using milk, mayonnaise—even banana peels. None of these are necessary if you dust your orchid's foliage on a regular basis.

Orchids with naturally shiny foliage, such as phalaenopsis, doritis, and green-leaved paphiopedilums, shine on their own when kept clean.

Other orchids have a matte finish to their leaves, lending them a natural beauty that chemicals can't improve.

Above left: **Residues from dust, fertilizer, and water can all mar the surface of normally shiny phalaenopsis leaves.**

Above center: **It's easy to keep orchid leaves clean with a quick polish from a soft cloth; even a soft sock will do. Don't let water sit on the foliage; it will leave residue.**

Above right: **The pleated foliage of this oncidium indicates that it has been unevenly watered at some point in its life. The leaf will never return to normal, even if proper watering is resumed.**

Root pruning

Scissors, floral snips, or pruners remove shriveled or rotten roots from orchids before repotting.

Orchid roots benefit from occasional pruning.

Once a year, it's worth knocking your orchids out of their pots to examine their roots.

Healthy roots of terrestrial orchids should be brown, thick, and hairy. If you find roots that are limp, black, and stringy, cut them off with sterilized scissors or pruners and repot the orchid.

Check roots of terrestrial orchids

Slimy roots are a definite sign of overwatering. It's easy to overwater terrestrial orchids when they're potted in plastic, because the plastic keeps the potting mix wetter longer.

Be sure to poke your finger down into the bark mix and feel for moisture before watering. If the mix feels dry an inch below the surface, it's time to water. But hold off if it's still wet.

Check the velamen on epiphytes

On epiphytes, healthy velamen roots are white and plump. If you see brown or black roots with wiry hairs sticking out of the ends, this is a sign of rot.

Cut back the dead roots with sterilized tools, then repot. If you've removed more than 10 percent of the root mass, reevaluate your watering pattern. It's possible you've been overwatering.

When you repot an epiphyte, let any roots that are growing upward remain outside the potting mix. Remember, epiphytes have aerial roots in nature, and while covering some with bark mix provides anchorage for the plant, it's a good idea to let the upward-growing roots preserve their natural habit and remain uncovered. Plus, they look cool!

TEST GARDEN TIP

Water the aerial roots

Rot isn't the only thing that kills orchid roots; aerial roots may die if they get too dry. If the exposed roots of your orchid are brittle rather than flexible and if they don't turn green when wet, they may be dead. When you water your orchid, be sure to moisten the aerial roots.

Left: **It's easy to tell the difference between the decayed, shriveled roots on the left and the healthy white roots on the right.**

Staking

Use a clip and stake to keep slender orchid stems upright and sturdy.

The most exciting part of growing orchids

is when you notice a new bloom spike emerging. Growers have been known to jump up and down and squeal like children at the sight of a swelling bud. It's the moment you've been waiting for, and you want to be sure to enjoy it.

It's not unusual for a bloom spike to be two or three times longer than the orchid is tall, and, as you can imagine, the weight of many flowers can cause the bloom spike to bend and droop.

Orchids that produce long sprays of flowers should be staked to create a graceful curve and to protect the spike from breaking.

Staking bloom spikes

When the bloom spike is about a foot tall but the buds have not yet opened, insert a slim stake, 14 to 15 inches tall, into the potting mix as close as possible to the bloom spike.

Twist the stake as you gently push it into the bark mix to avoid damaging roots. When the stake is in place, it should be about the same height as the bloom spike.

Using a twist tie, hook-and-loop tape, or miniclip, attach the bloom spike to the stake, allowing a little room for movement. Avoid wire or string and attach the tie loosely to keep the tie from cutting into the tissue of the stem.

For an attractive look, wrap a strip of sheet moss around the stem before applying the tie. This looks nice and protects the stem. Continue to tie or clip the spike to the stake every 3 or 4 inches, finishing an inch or two below the first bud. This style of staking supports the flower spike and still allows it to form a natural curve.

Keep budding orchids straight

Once buds have started to form on spray-type orchids or orchids with compact clusters of flowers, avoid changing the orientation of the plant to the light. The bloom spike grows toward the light, and flowers also open in this direction. Turning the plant while the spike is forming causes the stem to twist and turn, and flowers change their orientation. This distorts the elegance of a graceful curved stem full of flowers facing in a single direction.

When to hold off on staking

Miniature spray orchids and orchids with small clusters of two to four blooms (such as cattleyas) don't usually require staking.

Some orchid blooms should not be staked. Gongoras and stanhopeas, as well as trailing cymbidiums, produce flower spikes that cascade downward, hanging below the plant itself. The beauty of these blooms is best appreciated when the plants are suspended, permitting their flowers to dangle.

Stanhopeas are often grown in slatted boxes, allowing the bloom spikes to grow through the bottom of the container.

Trailing cymbidiums are usually grown in pots that should be placed on a high shelf or hung where flowers are at the optimum angle and height for appreciation.

TEST GARDEN TIP
DIY bloom spike

Bloom spikes are slightly flexible, which means you can get creative when you stake them. Choose a curve or angle for the spike that suits both the plant and the plant's location. When the orchid is displayed in a narrow alcove, an upright bloom stem might be best. Against a large blank wall, you may choose to stake your bloom spike in a wide arc or curve.

Left: **When the bloom spike of a phalaenopsis orchid begins growing, avoid turning the orchid toward the light source. Doing so results in a crooked stem.**

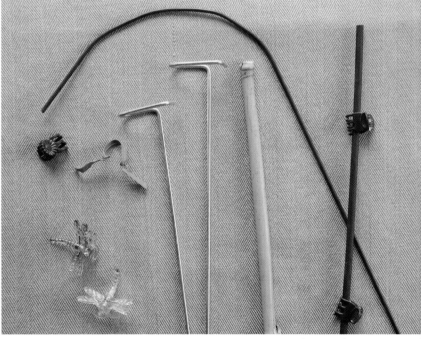

Above: **Keep a variety of stakes and clips on hand to support orchid stems. Straight sticks or metal rods are great for slipper orchids, while a curved stake is helpful with phalaenopsis.**

Deadheading

The first blooms to fade on a phalaenopsis orchid are usually the ones lowest on the stem, since they were the first buds to open.

In an outdoor garden, flowers are deadheaded to prevent the plant from using energy to ripen seeds and to encourage it to produce more flowers.

Since most orchids grown indoors remain unpollinated, deadheading is done only for aesthetic reasons. The flowers on a multibloom spike usually open from the bottom up. The older flowers, toward the bottom of the bloom spike, fade first.

Remove the flowers as they wilt by cutting each bloom as close as possible to the spike. With conscientious deadheading, you can keep a phalaenopsis looking fresh and new for several months.

Other orchids also produce multiple blooms that last for weeks, although none is quite as long lasting as the phalaenopsis.

Pruning the spike to rebloom phalaenopsis

When all the flowers have faded from your orchids, it's time to prune the bloom spike. On most orchids, cut the spike back to its point of origin. This is either at the top of a pseudobulb or at a node on a cane or stem.

With strategic pruning, phalaenopsis orchids can often be persuaded to produce another full spike of blooms. They are the only orchids that grow this way.

Notice the white nodes that mark the bloom spike at regular intervals. Count up three or four nodes from the bottom and make a cut directly above the third or fourth node.

About half the time a new bloom spike will emerge from the node immediately below the cut. It's a great way to get more bloom from your phalaenopsis, but after forcing a spike, let your plant rest so it can focus its energy on root and foliage growth.

TEST GARDEN TIP

Using orchids as cut flowers

The orchids that bloom longest as plants also produce the longest-lasting cut flowers. A stem of phalaenopsis blooms can look fresh and lovely for three weeks. Cymbidium flowers are also long lasting. Be sure to change the water in your vase every five to seven days for optimum bloom longevity.

A snip in time Scissors or floral snips come in handy when grooming your orchids. These techniques are especially valuable for phalaenopsis, also known as moth orchids.

REMOVE SPENT FLOWERS Fading flowers eventually fall off an orchid on their own, but they'll look tired for a long while before they do that. Just clip at the base of the bloom to immediately improve the looks of your phalaenopsis.

CUT ABOVE A NODE You can clearly identify the branch nodes on a phalaenopsis orchid. When all of the flowers on a bloom spike have finished blooming, make a clean cut just above the node and discard the old bloomed-out stem.

REGROW A NEW BLOOM SPIKE Sometimes a new spike will grow from the node, eventually forming buds that burst into flowers. Do this just once per spike; give your plant time to rejuvenate itself.

Repotting

The old, decayed potting mix on the left has smaller particles than the fresh, new mix on the right.

How do you know when it's time to repot your orchid?

Plants should be repotted every few years for a variety of reasons: The potting mix needs to be refreshed; overgrown sympodial orchids may benefit from division; aging monopodial orchids need pruning; and offshoots can be removed and potted up on their own.

As bark mix biodegrades, the particles become smaller and drainage slows. Old, broken-down mix may hold too much water, leading to root rot.

Check every year

Has it been more than a year since you've repotted your orchid? Take an objective look at your potting mix. If the particles look considerably smaller than they did when you first got the plant, that's a sign of biodegradation.

Does the potting mix take longer to drain than it used to? Does it smell musty, fungal, or otherwise damp and moldy? If the bark no longer smells fresh and woody, it's time to repot. As potting mix ages, it becomes more compact and aeration decreases, meaning the orchids' roots have less exposure to the air.

The higher the moisture and temperature, the faster the mix breaks down. Bark mix breaks down faster in plastic pots than it does in clay pots because of increased moisture.

Repotting can vary

Depending on the frequency of watering and the type of pot you're using, orchids should be repotted every one to two years to refresh nutrients and ensure roots get the aeration and quick drainage they require.

If you keep your orchids on the dry side, you may not need to repot more than once in three years.

On the other hand, if you grow orchids that need constant moisture (such as miltonias, phragmipediums, and paphiopedilums), you may need to replace the bark mix more often.

Inorganic potting mixes break down much more slowly and require less-frequent refreshing. However, they are more expensive and provide no nutrition to your plants.

When to repot

Repot phalaenopsis orchids every other year, immediately after they finish blooming.

Sympodial orchids such as dendrobiums and oncidiums should be repotted when you see the first signs of active root growth. New leaves and pseudobulbs usually precede new roots, so look at the base of new top growth to see if roots have started to grow. If you find the beginning of new roots, your timing is just right.

Active growth for orchids usually begins in late spring to early summer, the perfect time to repot. Avoid summer, because high temperatures can add to the stress of transplanting. Repotting during short, cold winter days mean the plants won't establish themselves as quickly as they should.

TEST GARDEN TIP

When to repot

Replace or refresh potting mix every two years or so, depending on growing conditions and maintenance habits.

Left: **Circling roots and dark, decaying potting mix indicate it's time to repot an orchid.**

Dividing orchids with multiple growing points

This cymbidium orchid will soon outgrow its pot and need to be divided. Using a tall pot helps visually balance the very long leaves.

Often, it's necessary to divide an orchid before repotting.

Symodial orchids with more than one growing point, such as dendrobiums and oncidiums, grow horizontally across a pot. When they fill the available space, they continue to grow out and over the edge.

You have a choice: Move the orchid as a whole to a larger pot, or divide it into two or more pieces and repot each one in a smaller container.

Transplant the entire orchid to a larger pot for any of these reasons: If you have room for a bigger pot in your growing area; if you like the idea of a large specimen plant; or if the entire plant is leafy and productive. As with any potted plant, make sure you maintain the original potting level, planting the orchid no deeper or shallower than it was in its previous container.

It's better to divide and repot, however, if your growing space couldn't possibly accommodate a larger pot or you have a friend who's been eyeing the plant and hinting how much she wants a piece or if several of the pseudobulbs or canes have lost their foliage. This not only makes your friend happy, but it also rejuvenates the orchid.

Remove the orchid from its pot

Be careful! New root growth is delicate and must be handled gently. Start by tapping the orchid out of its container. Sometimes this is easy. Just tip the pot upside down, and the orchid slides out into your hand.

If the roots have grown onto the container wall, run a knife around the inside of the pot to break the connection between roots and container.

However, if the roots have grown onto the pot so extensively that you can't remove them without serious damage, gently break the pot into pieces, allowing any pot shards left attached to the roots to remain connected. Remove as much of the old bark mix as possible from the orchid's roots and take a look at the root ball. If you see any dead roots, snip them off before repotting your plant.

How many divisions to make

Now take a look at your plant. Count how many pseudobulbs or canes there are. When dividing a symodial orchid, each division should have at least three bulbs or canes. Smaller divisions may not be able to store or produce adequate nutrition for vigorous growth.

Use sterilized pruners to cut through the rhizome that connects the pseudobulbs or canes at their bases. You may, for example, come up with two divisions of four active pseudobulbs each, and one division with three backbulbs (older pseudobulbs that have lost their foliage).

ASK THE GARDEN DOCTOR

Sphagnum moss or bark mix?

ANSWER: If you tend to underwater your plants, consider leaving your orchids in moss. If you tend to overwater plants, repot from sphagnum to bark mix.

Dividing sympodials

All sympodial orchids, not just the cymbidium shown below, can be divided and repotted using these techniques.

1 DIVIDE
Begin by pulling the large root ball into pieces, gently teasing the roots apart. If the roots won't move, carefully use pruners to help.

2 GROOM
Using pruners or scissors, trim away any dead roots, leaf sheaths, and inactive backbulbs.

3 PLACE
Add bark mix to the bottom of the pot, then place the division with the older bulbs against one side of the pot.

4 FILL
Holding the division in place, add bark mix to the pot, carefully tamping it into open crevices with your fingers or a thin tool.

Repotting orchids with multiple growing points

Choose new pots for your divisions.

Symodial orchids—which have several growing points—should have a larger pot-to-root ratio than those with a single growing point (monopodials) because sympodial orchids grow horizontally. Examine the existing growth and visualize how large the orchid will be with two to four additional pseudobulbs. That's how large the pot should be. Plan for enough extra space across the top of the pot to hold two years' growth.

If each division is 4 inches in diameter at the base, for example, you'll need a 6-inch pot for each plant. Add a layer of bark mix to the bottom of the pot, enough to maintain the orchid at its original potting depth.

How to replant

Place the orchid division so that the oldest pseudobulb is flush against the wall of the pot. Since growth proceeds outward from the newest pseudobulb, this gives your orchid maximum room to grow.

Holding the orchid in place with one hand, use the other to place bark mix in and around the roots of your orchid, poking and pressing it tightly

Above: **The many stems of this paphiopedilum are growing from horizontal rhizomes in the potting mix.**

into place. Unless you use pressure to force the bark mix in and among the roots, the orchid may fall out of the pot as soon as you let go.

Even when the bark is properly arranged, you may need to use a rhizome clip to keep the plant upright while its roots grow in. Plastic and clay pots require different styles of clips, but both are inexpensive. Attach the clip to the edge of the pot with the horizontal bar running across the rhizome. Downward pressure holds the orchid firmly in place.

Rejuvenating backbulbs

If you're feeling adventurous, try kickstarting your leafless backbulbs into active growth. You have nothing to lose. This works especially well with oncidium and cymbidium orchids.

Separate the backbulbs from one another, clean the bark mix from the roots, then trim off any dead root material. In a large plastic sandwich or quart-size bag, spread a layer of moist sphagnum moss about 2 inches deep. The moss should be damp, but should not drip water if you squeeze a bunch of it in your hand.

Place the backbulbs in the sphagnum moss, covering the bottom inch of each bulb, then seal the bag. Leave the bag in a warm spot (about 70°F) in bright, but not direct, light. In about two months, you should see new foliage sprouting from some (probably not all) of the bulbs.

Move any rooted pseudobulbs that have new foliage into a small pot with bark mix and let them all grow together for another few months. When new pseudobulbs appear, you can repot, if desired.

TEST GARDEN TIP

Sterilize pruners

Sterilize your pruners before working with a plant to prevent the spread of disease. Swipe the blade with rubbing alcohol or a 10 percent bleach solution. Or hold the blade of your cutting tool over a flame (such as a lighter) for a few seconds. If you choose the flame method, let the blade cool before using it.

Above left: **Place sympodial divisions against the side of a pot, to allow the walking habit of its roots to move in the opposite direction.**

Above right: **A rhizome clip helps hold an orchid division in place during potting. Leave it in place while the plant establishes itself in the new pot.**

Left: **Instead of tossing out leafless backbulbs, you can try rooting them in moist sphagnum moss in a plastic bag. The bag acts as a small, humid greenhouse, encouraging roots to grow.**

Repotting single growing point orchids

Wait to repot phalaenopsis orchids until after they have finished blooming. Otherwise, the stress to the plant is likely to kill the blooms.

Monopodial orchids, such as phalaenopsis and vandas,

can't be divided in the same way as sympodial orchids because they only have one growing point. However, they can be cleaned up and cut back to improve their looks and fit your growing space.

If you have a monopodial orchid that has outgrown its container and you have room for a bigger pot on your windowsill, you can simply transplant the orchid and grow it in a larger container.

Unlike a sympodial orchid, a monopodial orchid should be centered in the pot. When repotting monopodial orchids, fit the pot to the root system. The container should be large enough to accommodate the roots without a lot of scrunching, but small enough that the roots reach (or almost reach) the edges of the pot.

Topping a monopodial orchid

If your monopodial orchid has lost many of its lower leaves and shows several inches of

bare stem, and if the bare section of stem has produced aerial roots, you can try cutting off the top to make two plants.

Knock the orchid out of its pot, remove as much of the old bark mix as possible from the orchid's roots, and prune any dead roots using a sterilized pruner.

Cut the orchid stem about 2 inches below the lowest leaf, making sure to include several aerial roots on the portion of the stem above the cut. Pot the cutting in bark mix by first adding mix to the bottom of the pot, then holding the cutting in the center as you firmly press the bark nuggets around the stem and roots. The level of bark mix should reach to just below the first leaf.

Because the new cutting lacks an extensive root system, give it extra humidity with a dry well or humidity tray.

You can also repot the bottom section. In many instances it, too, will sprout new leaves.

Above left: **To repot a phalaenopis that has been planted in sphagnum moss, carefully remove the moss from the roots, then cut out any dead or shriveled parts.**

Above center: **Center the phalaenopsis in the pot, using a fine bark mix that's appropriate for a smaller plant. The eraser end of a pencil is a handy tool to coax the bark into spaces between the roots.**

Above right: **The repotted phalaenopsis now lives in a better-draining bark mix in a clay pot that's designed with slits to provide air circulation.**

Potting offshoots

Some orchids reproduce in much the same way that Athena sprang from the head of her father, Zeus, in the mythic story—that is, the offshoot emerges directly from the body of the parent.

These offshoots are called "keikis," which is the Hawaiian word meaning "babies." Keiki is pronounced "kay-kee." They are most commonly found growing from the bloom spikes of phalaenopsis and vanda orchids and from nodes on dendrobium canes.

Keikis should be left on the parent plant until enough roots develop for the young plant to be potted on its own: from four to six roots that are 2 to 3 inches long.

You may leave the keiki on the parent plant, if you like how it looks. It's entirely possible for the keiki to bloom while still attached to its parent.

If you want to make more plants, remove the keiki by cutting (with sterilized pruners) just below the new roots for both types of orchids. With a monopodial, cut below the new roots and above the top leaf.

Place it in a small pot that's just large enough to accommodate the young roots.

Freshly potted keikis require extra humidity while their root systems become established in the new potting mix. You may also need to stake them for the first few months.

Above left: **Dendrobiums, such as Burana Angel 'Blue', often produce keikis that grow along their canes.**

Above right: **Keikis are also frequently produced on phalaenopsis orchids, but may emerge above the parent.**

Offshoots from monopodial orchids
Single-growing-point phalaenopsis may produce keikis above the parent plant. You can either leave them attached, or give each keiki its own pot.

1 CUT
Decide whether you want to remove the keiki from the parent plant or let it grow. It's easy to remove a phalaenopsis keiki: Snip the stem that attaches it to its parent as well as the stem above it.

2 REPOT
Place the keiki's roots into a pot and continue filling the spaces with fresh bark mix as you would repotting any orchid.

Offshoots from sympodial orchids
If the hairy look of the white-rooted offshoots growing from orchids such as dendrobiums is not attractive to you, follow these steps.

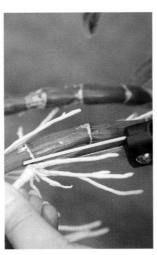

1 SELECT
Decide which keikis have long-enough roots to divide from the parent cane.

2 SNIP
Without damaging the parent cane, carefully cut the keiki off.

3 POT
Center the keiki so the roots can run in all directions, then fill with bark mix.

4 STAKE
Support the tender keiki with a stake and twist tie, and add a label.

Special planting considerations

Because slipper orchids (paphiopedilums) prefer to have their potting medium remain slightly moist at all times, sphagnum moss is a good choice.

You may have seen orchids potted in glass vases

that are lined with sphagnum or sheet moss. It's an attractive way to display a plant, but not a practical one.

Since these vases lack drainage holes, excess water can't escape, and many people simply fill up the vase with water, not realizing they are drowning their plant.

How to water glass-potted orchids

If you like the look and want to keep your orchid in glass, there's a specific way to water it. Take your orchid to the sink and fill the vase with water. Let the water sit for 5 to 10 minutes.

Then, spreading your fingers across the entire top of the vase and around the base of the orchid, tip the vase upside down, draining the excess, unabsorbed water. When the water stops dripping, turn the vase right side up, and return the orchid to its place.

Orchids potted in glass dry out slowly, so use the finger test (or a moisture meter designed for orchids) and avoid watering if the potting mix is still moist. It may be 10 days or longer before the orchid needs water again.

Repot in bark mix if you overwater

If you buy an orchid potted in long-grain sphagnum but know you tend to overwater, repot it into bark mix.

When the orchid finishes blooming, gently knock it out of its pot and remove as much of the sphagnum moss as possible. Soaking the root ball in water makes the moss easier to get off. It's OK if you can't remove every last strand; just do the best you can.

Repot the orchid in bark mix. If it's a monopodial orchid, such as a phalaenopsis, center it in the pot. If it's sympodial, such as a dendrobium or oncidium, place the old growth against the pot wall.

You might want to leave a phragmipedium or paphiopedilum (slipper orchid) potted in sphagnum moss or fine bark because those orchids appreciate more consistent moisture.

TEST GARDEN TIP

Orchids age well

Older orchids may produce both more flowers and more spikes than they did when they were young, although the more flowers a bloom stem bears, the smaller those flowers are likely to be.

Left: **If you plant a paphiopedilum in a bark mix, be sure to use a fine-grain mix, which holds more moisture than a coarse-grain mix.**

Above: **Be careful not to overwater a phalaenopsis planted in sphagnum moss in a glass container. Both retain moisture that can lead to rotted roots.**

keeping orchids healthy

Keeping orchids healthy isn't complicated. Start with clean plants and keep a close eye on them. Early detection and treatment are keys to controlling pests and diseases.

p.96
TROUBLESHOOTING

Yellow leaves? No bloom? Check this section for answers, including which orchid to grow if your pet likes to nibble.

p.98
PESTS & DISEASES

Prevention is the best defense against pests and diseases. Learn how to spot the signals that tell when your orchid is in trouble.

p.104
PHYSICAL DAMAGE

Orchids will tell you when something is wrong. Leaves go brown or yellow, pseudobulbs shrivel, and flowers refuse to open.

p.106
CREATING AN ORCHID HOSPITAL

Orchids may need intensive care. Give them some TLC with your own orchid ICU.

Troubleshooting

Yellow leaves
Leaf yellowing can mean several things.

TOO MUCH LIGHT
If your orchid is getting too much light, the foliage may turn yellowish. Match your orchid to its profile in the Gallery of Orchids, starting on page 130 and, if indicated, adjust the amount of light it gets.

OVERWATERING
Yellow leaves may indicate overwatering. If your orchid likes to dry out between waterings, adjust the watering schedule to keep your orchid from rotting.

NITROGEN DEFICIENCY
Yellow leaves may also be a sign of a nitrogen deficiency. You may need to increase the frequency of feeding—but never increase the concentration of fertilizer beyond what's suggested on the plant-food container. An application that's too strong could burn the roots and kill the plant.

Twisted bloom spike
Ideally, the bloom spike of a phalaenopsis orchid should arch gracefully and the flowers should all face in the same direction.

This can only be accomplished if the orchid is left in the same position relative to its light source from the time the bloom spike emerges.

LEAVE PLANT IN PLACE
When you move your orchid in order to water or feed it, be sure to place it back the same way it was facing before. If you change its orientation, the stem will turn to face the light source, causing it to twist and the flowers to grow in several different directions. You will lose the graceful, simple shape of the arching bloom spike.

Brown leaf tips
Browning on leaf margins and tips can be the result of fertilizer burn or arid conditions.

TOO MUCH FERTILIZER
When too much fertilizer burns an orchid's roots, the first visible signs are brown leaf tips and margins. The damaged tissue will never turn green again. Correct your tendency to overfeed and trim the leaves to imitate their natural shape.

TOO DRY
If the air surrounding your orchid's leaves is too dry, leaf margins may turn brown as water evaporates from leaf tissue more rapidly than it can be replaced. Place your orchid on a dry well and trim off the brown margins.

No blooms
If your orchid doesn't bloom, ask these questions, in this order:

DO NIGHTTIME TEMPERATURES DROP?
In nature, nighttime temperatures are generally 10 to 15°F lower than daytime temperatures. Some orchids require this temperature difference to set buds. If you summer your orchids outdoors, you should be able to provide this difference naturally. Indoors, windowsills are your best bet. Use a minimum-maximum thermometer to assess your situation.

IS IT GETTING ENOUGH LIGHT?
Orchids produce healthy foliage in lower light than they require to bloom. If the leaves look healthy but you have no flowers, check the light level of your growing location. Chances are the orchid needs more light.

IS IT TOO WET?
Some orchids require a dry period to trigger bloom. This relates to their natural bloom period, which generally follows a dormant, dry season. Check the requirements for your orchid to see if it responds to a dry rest.

Root rot
You've just knocked your orchid out of its pot, and it's not a pretty sight. Most of the roots have rotted, and after trimming away the shriveled, useless dead roots, you have only two or three living roots left to support the entire plant. Can your orchid survive?

ANSWER:
Maybe. Repot your plant in an appropriate-size pot (probably smaller than the one it was in, since it no longer has many roots) and fresh, premoistened bark mix. Since the small number of remaining roots can't provide enough moisture to keep the plant healthy, you'll need to compensate by raising the ambient humidity. Place the entire pot in a mini greenhouse. It can be anything from a dry cleaner's bag to an aquarium tank to a bell jar. This will slow the loss of water via transpiration and give your orchid a fighting chance.

Orchid selection
Not everyone can grow every orchid. If you select orchids based on your growing environment and the kind of care you can realistically give, you'll be taking an important first step. Consider your lifestyle to make the right choices about which orchid to grow. Here are some helpful suggestions:

I TEND TO OVERWATER:
Phaphiopedilum, phragmipedium

I SOMETIMES IGNORE MY PLANTS:
Cattleya, oncidium, dendrobium

I KEEP MY HOUSE COOL:
Cymbidium, odontoglossum, masdevallia

I KEEP MY HOUSE WARM:
Vanda, phalaenopsis, angraecum

THE AIR IN MY HOUSE IS DRY:
Cattleya, dendrobium

MY HOME IS DARK:
Jewel orchids, paphiopedilum

I ONLY HAVE A SMALL WINDOWSILL:
Minicattleya, masdevallia, pleurothallis, miniature phalaenopsis

I DON'T UNDERSTAND FERTILIZERS:
Phalaenopsis, cattleya

I'M AFRAID OF GROWING ORCHIDS:
Phalaenopsis, dendrobium

I WANT TO MOVE MY ORCHIDS OUTSIDE IN SUMMER:
Vanda, cymbidium, cattleya

MY PET EATS MY PLANTS:
Phalaenopsis, cattleya, vanda (thick-leafed plants that pets avoid)

Dealing with pests

Remedies Pest prevention is better than treatment. The best way to minimize pest problems in your orchid collection is to be vigilant. Before buying an orchid, check thoroughly under leaves, between pseudobulbs, and inside flowers for signs of infestation.

ISOLATE

Juvenile insects can be hard to see, so when you bring a new orchid home, keep it isolated for a few weeks before integrating it into your collection to be sure it's clean. Every time you water, examine your plants for signs of pest predation such as sticky spots on leaves, webs in leaf axils, and holes in foliage.

SANITIZE

Sanitation is extremely important in minimizing pest damage. Insects and mites may hide on the undersides of leaves or lie dormant in potting mix. If you find a problem, take extra care to clean the growing area, getting rid of any plant debris and thoroughly cleaning all surfaces with a weak bleach solution.

REMOVE

Physical removal is an excellent, nontoxic pest control method. As soon as you spot a pest problem, remove the pests. If the infestation is severe, remove the entire affected part of the plant.

Tools Have a few tools and home remedies on hand so you can spring into action if you find insects on your orchids.

MAGNIFY

A magnifying glass or loupe is helpful for spotting pests, especially tiny spider mites.

SWAB

Keep cotton swabs and cotton balls on hand to apply rubbing alcohol to control mealybugs and scale.

SPRAY AND SOAK

A spray bottle is useful for dealing with aphids and fungus gnats. A plastic washbasin 6 to 8 inches deep can be used to prepare soaking solutions so you can leave plants dripping without cluttering up the sink. When there's only one plant to spray, doing it in a basin in the sink is a good way to minimize cleanup.

Ants Although ants themselves aren't actually orchid pests, if you see them on your plants it's a good indication you may have an underlying problem.

SIGNS

Ants act as shepherds for several types of leaf-piercing and sucking insects, including aphids, scale, and mealybugs. They carry young insects from plant to plant, defend them from predators, and collect the insects' excretions that are rich in sugars and a valuable food for ants.

DAMAGE

None, but they are indicators of a problem.

PREVENTION AND MANAGEMENT

If you notice ants on your orchids, pull out your magnifying glass for a closer look. You'll probably find an additional insect problem.

Scale
This pest doesn't look like an insect so it's easy to miss.

SIGNS

Scale looks like small brown or tan bumps on a leaf or stem. Beneath a protective covering, a soft-bodied insect sucks nutrients from plant leaves.

DAMAGE

Scale cluster on the undersides of leaves, along midribs, or in the papery sheaths at the bases of pseudobulbs. Scale insects suck sugars from foliage. This produces dead tissue, which distorts the plant and impedes its ability to photosynthesize. The sticky honeydew that scale excrete can host sooty mold. Leaves damaged by scale eventually yellow and fall off, and the plant may die.

PREVENTION AND MANAGEMENT

Because of its protective covering, scale is tough to kill. Soap-based spray kills juveniles, but you must eradicate adults by removing them or smothering them with an oil-based product. Watering with a systemic poison solution makes the plant poisonous not only to the insects but also to pets or children. Instead, scrub off scale with a cotton swab soaked in alcohol. Spray the plant with a solution made of 1 part dishwashing liquid, 1 part mineral oil, and 8 parts water. Continue as needed until the plant is clean for four weeks.

Mealybugs
A type of soft scale, mealybugs are covered with white cottony material instead of an inflexible brown shell. Like scale, they don't look like insects, so you may overlook them until their population has grown to dangerous proportions.

SIGNS

Look for a cottony coat, the waxy excretion that protects them from traditional insecticides, except when they are at the juvenile crawler stage. Also like scale, they excrete honeydew, which provides sooty mold with a place to grow.

DAMAGE

Mealybug saliva may cause leaf distortion and death. Mealybugs collect in leaf axils, between pseudobulbs, and underneath the sheaths found at the bases of pseudobulbs and canes. Some mealybugs live among and feed on plant roots.

PREVENTION AND MANAGEMENT

A cotton swab soaked in alcohol dissolves mealybugs' protective covering, revealing and killing the soft-bodied pink insects beneath. Oil-based sprays smother and kill the insects at all stages, and soap sprays kill unprotected juveniles.

Aphids
Sticky honeydew is one sign of aphids, but unlike scale and mealybugs they have no protective coverings so they're easier to kill.

SIGNS

Aphids often cluster on the tender buds of orchid plants, making them difficult to eradicate. You should avoid using harsh sprays on a bud or handling the bud roughly when physically removing aphids for fear of sacrificing bloom. Aphids multiply quickly and come in many colors: orange, green, black, white, brown, yellow, or pink.

DAMAGE

Aphids are sucking insects; they pierce leaf tissue with their mouthparts, taking nutrition from orchid leaves, leaving behind stunted plants and distorted or dead tissue. They also spread diseases.

PREVENTION AND MANAGEMENT

If aphids are on delicate tissue, like a bud or flower, use fingers coated with dishwashing liquid to gently remove the insects from the plant. (You can wear latex gloves if you wish.) If they are on foliage, use a sharp spray of water to blast them off. Once you've physically removed all visible aphids, spray the plant with a solution of 10 percent dishwashing liquid. Repeat every three to four days until two weeks pass without seeing any aphids.

Pests & diseases

Spider mites
Their tiny size makes spider mites difficult to spot. Because they're arachnids, insecticides don't work.

SIGNS
If you suspect spider mites, mist the plant with water. Droplets caught in the webbing make an infestation clearly visible.

DAMAGE
Spider mites are sucking pests that can quickly damage a leaf. Leaf surfaces become mottled and dimpled and the undersides may look silvery. Foliage eventually turns yellow, then falls off. Spider mites thrive in dry heat and reproduce quickly. They travel easily from plant to plant, sometimes hitching a ride on your tools, hands, or clothing.

PREVENTION AND MANAGEMENT
Isolate the orchid and wash your hands before working on the next plant. Although you can use chemicals, it's not wise indoors. Fill a plastic basin with 4 inches of cold water. Swirl in a few squirts of dishwashing liquid and several capfuls of mineral oil. Use one hand to hold the bark mix in place and the other to swish the leaves in the liquid. Coat both sides of every leaf. Let suds sit on the leaves for 15 to 20 minutes, then rinse with cold water. Repeat every five to seven days until you go a month without seeing mites.

Fungus gnats
Adult fungus gnats look like fruit flies. Their larvae feed on the organic matter in potting mix.

SIGNS
You can't see fungus gnats feeding on plant parts. Instead you'll see them crawling on bark mix or hovering around the plant.

DAMAGE
Orchid roots count as organic material, and fungus gnat larvae not only feed on roots, but can also transmit diseases, including several fungal diseases that can kill an orchid.

PREVENTION AND MANAGEMENT
Fungus gnats can be controlled fairly easily by letting potting mix dry out between waterings. Since many orchids are drought-tolerant, you should be able to keep the potting mix on the dry side for several weeks and interrupt the fungus gnats' life cycle. If you're growing orchids that require a moist potting mix (miltonias, paphiopedilums, phragmipediums) and can't let the potting mix dry thoroughly, try spraying with neem oil, which acts against insects in several ways. It suppresses feeding and also interrupts the insects' life cycle, making it impossible for them to reproduce.

Slugs
If you move your orchids outside in summer, or purchase them from a large commercial greenhouse, it's entirely possible to bring slugs indoors.

SIGNS
There's no missing a fat, slippery slug when you find one on your orchid. Young slugs are easier to miss. They can be smaller than a centimeter and will curl up in a ball in an effort to escape detection.

DAMAGE
Slugs can stay hidden between pieces of bark mix during the day, slithering out at night to feast on orchid foliage and flowers, leaving behind silvery trails and mangled leaves.

PREVENTION AND MANAGEMENT
Slugs don't reproduce as fast as insect and arachnid pests, so you should be able to pick them off by hand. First thing in the morning, inspect your pots, removing any slugs you find. You can control slugs by decreasing moisture in your potting mix. Though there are several chemical slug controls on the market, they probably aren't necessary for what is a minor pest to the home orchid grower.

Disease remedies
As with pests, it's better to avoid diseases than to do battle with them.

INSPECT

Inspect new orchids thoroughly for signs of disease like spots and soft patches. If you find something suspicious, resist the temptation to nurse the orchid back to health. You're better off starting with a healthy specimen.

LEARN

Most plant diseases are caused by pathogens such as fungi, bacteria, or viruses. Pathogens enter plants through openings in their epidermis. Water containing pathogens may splash onto a leaf's surface and enter through a wound or stomata (leaf pores). Insects can transmit disease by spreading pathogens during feeding. Humans transport pathogens by using the same pruners on an infected plant and a healthy one. Sterilize your blades or use one single-edge razor blade per orchid.

TREAT

Cutting diseased tissue is a good first step, but sometimes you must treat healthy tissue as a preventive measure. Cinnamon is an excellent fungicide and has some antibacterial properties. It's safe to use in the home and is probably something you already have on hand. Sprinkle it onto the cut. If you need something stronger, use Physan 20, a broad-spectrum fungicide-bactericide.

Tools
Most diseases can be prevented by providing clean conditions and taking conscientious care of your orchids. A few simple tools help with that.

CIRCULATE

A small muffin fan (found at well-stocked hardware stores and electrical supply houses) improves circulation and speeds the evaporation of standing water where pathogens can thrive. You can use any small desk fan as a substitute.

CUT

Use floral snips or pruners to physically remove any diseased plant part and restrict the spread of disease. Sterilize your tool to avoid carrying disease from one plant to another.

MEDICATE

Use a mister to spray fungicide or bactericide on the diseased plant after surgery. Cinnamon can be sprinkled directly onto the wound in powder form.

Botrytis
One of the most easily recognizable plant fungi, botrytis is also referred to as gray mold or flower blight. On orchids, botrytis shows up on flowers as small brown or black flecks that become larger and more numerous as the infection grows. While botrytis won't kill your plant, it spoils the beauty of the bloom.

DAMAGE

As the disease develops and spores increase in numbers, they form a gray, fuzzy mass that is easily spread by the slightest movement.

PREVENTION AND MANAGEMENT

Remove any visibly infected plant parts immediately and examine your watering practices. Standing water left on orchid leaves or petals provides excellent growing conditions for botrytis spores when combined with 60°F temperature. Poor air circulation encourages the fungus to grow. Orchids growing outdoors usually get enough natural air circulation to prevent the disease, but in greenhouses and homes, air can be stagnant. Adding a small fan to your growing area improves circulation. Water early in the day so any excess can evaporate before temperatures drop in the evening. Botrytis is a common fungus, but by improving the growing conditions you can make your plants inhospitable to spore growth.

Diseases

Sooty mold A black, grainy fungus that sticks to honeydew and spreads over the surface of a leaf, sooty mold grows in the honeydew, the excrement of several types of sucking insects.

DAMAGE

Not only is it unattractive and indicative of an insect problem, but the mold also interferes with photosynthesis, since it blocks light from entering the leaf's chlorophyll.

PREVENTION AND MANAGEMENT

Sooty mold is easy to get rid of. Because it doesn't penetrate leaf tissue, you can wash it off with soap and water. However, if you don't address the underlying insect problem that's creating the honeydew, the sooty mold will regrow. If you find it on your orchids, use a magnifying glass to look for insects. Get rid of the pests to solve the problem.

Black rot The name black rot sounds ominous, and it is. Black rot can kill an orchid quickly and spreads easily from plant to plant.

DAMAGE

Black rot is caused by two fungi—*Pythium ultimum* and *Phytophthora cactorum*—that thrive in standing water. The fungi attack a wide range of orchids, but cattleyas are especially susceptible. Black rot spores can swim, and if they are splashed on leaf tissue, can grow in the leaf. The fungi produce brown spots that turn black, rapidly covering leaves. The spots turn soft and watery. Infection spreads when water splashes from an affected area to a healthy orchid or through contact with contaminated tools.

PREVENTION AND MANAGEMENT

Good air circulation is an excellent preventive for all fungal diseases. Water early in the day and eliminate any standing water. If you discover black rot, isolate the plant. Use a sterile cutting tool to remove the diseased section, leaving a clean margin of ½ to 1 inch. Examine the interior of the orchid. A plant can look healthy and green on the outside but show the beginning signs of rot (brown discoloration) on the inside. When margins are clean, sprinkle cinnamon—a safe and natural fungicide—onto the cut.

Bacterial brown rot Two bacteria cause brown rot and brown spot of orchids. *Pseudomonas* causes sunken black or brown spots on orchid foliage. It's most common on phalaenopsis. Rot caused by *Erwinia* most often affects paphiopedilum orchids.

DAMAGE

Pseudomonas spots are soft and watery and spread quickly to take over the entire leaf. *Erwinia* brown leaf spots also advance quickly and have a distinctive, pungent smell.

PREVENTION AND MANAGEMENT

A speedy diagnosis is required for brown rot and brown spot because they progress quickly. Both diseases thrive in humid conditions, especially when orchid foliage is left wet. Watering early in the day and improving air circulation minimize bacterial brown rot and spot. Avoid leaving standing water on orchid foliage. Use the bactericide Physan 20 for both diseases. Remove the affected plant part or parts, cutting slightly deeper than the damaged tissue for clean margins. Spray with Physan, then spray again in three to four days. While cinnamon has some antibacterial properties, it probably wouldn't work fast enough to stop bacterial brown rot or brown spot.

Leaf spot
Other leaf spot diseases are caused by a variety of fungi: *Cercospora*, *Phyllosticta*, and *Septoria*.

DAMAGE
These fungi aren't usually fatal, but left untreated, they cause foliage to drop. However, these diseases spread so slowly that there is no excuse for letting them win.

PREVENTION AND MANAGEMENT
If you provide clean growing conditions and good air circulation, and allow no standing water on orchid foliage, you should be able to avoid the minor leaf spot diseases. The spots, once established, do not go away, so you may want to trim the foliage to improve your plant's appearance. If you can't seem to break the life cycle of the fungi, incorporate a monthly preventive fungicide spray into your care and maintenance schedule.

Crown rot
The name refers to the location of the disease, not the fungi and bacteria that cause it. Crown rot is devastating for monopodial orchids that have only one growing point. A sympodial orchid with several growing points or crowns may be saved, but quick, decisive action is essential. Remove affected plants to prevent spreading the disease.

DAMAGE
Rot occurs when water is left standing in the crown of an orchid. In nature, epiphytic orchids grow on trees at angles that don't allow water to stay in the crown. Orchids in containers, however, easily catch and hold water. Standing water and cool temperatures form a breeding ground for fungi and bacteria. Orchids may develop crown rot when improperly potted too deeply in long-grain sphagnum moss that's kept constantly wet. Misting orchids can lead to droplets that run down leaves and collect in the crowns. Yellow foliage turns mushy, then black, then falls off. An orchid without leaves will have a difficult time growing new ones.

PREVENTION AND MANAGEMENT
Check the crowns of your plants—especially phalaenopsis—after watering to be sure there is no water left standing. If there is, gently absorb the water with a paper towel.

Viruses
No cure exists for virus diseases. Fortunately, they are relatively rare and it's entirely possible you may never have to deal with a virused plant.

DAMAGE
The most common viruses among orchids are cymbidium mosaic virus and odontoglossum ringspot virus. They can cause sunken spots on leaf and flower tissue or irregular colored streaks on flowers. They may also cause no visible symptoms, but merely decrease the vigor of a plant. Viruses can be transmitted from plant to plant by pests, human handling, or reusing contaminated potting mix or containers. Because a plant can carry a virus and be symptom-free, it's not always possible to know if you have a sick plant. This underlines the importance of always using sterile practices when working with your orchids.

PREVENTION AND MANAGEMENT
The best way to avoid bringing virused plants into your collection is to buy from a grower who guarantees virus-free stock. Some growers won't do this, so be sure to ask. You can buy at-home virus test kits or send plant samples out for laboratory testing if you suspect a virus—but why bother? Let the grower take care of that.

Physical damage

Cold damage
Cold temperatures cause severe injury and may even kill orchids. Because the symptoms take several days to become visible, it's possible to buy an orchid that has been injured and not realize this is the case. Orchids purchased in winter should be closely examined for signs of cold damage.

DAMAGE
Cold damage manifests in several ways that aren't always easy to interpret. Watery, sunken spots may develop on leaves. Brown or black spots may appear on foliage, or leaves may turn yellow, mushy, and fall off. Buds blast. Many of these symptoms resemble those of fungal and bacterial diseases, so it's not always easy to figure out what went wrong. You may bring home an orchid that looks healthy only to watch it disintegrate.

PREVENTION AND MANAGEMENT
In winter, take a cooler when you go shopping. The cooler's insulation protects orchids from cold damage for a few hours. If you're walking a short distance, you won't need a cooler, but it's a good idea to wrap the orchid in a paper or plastic sleeve or shopping bag. A cymbidium can handle temperatures in the 40°F range, while a phalaenopsis in bud shouldn't get below 65°F.

Heat stress
Extreme heat is just as dangerous to orchids as extreme cold. This surprises people who think of orchids as exotic tropicals that need constant high temperatures. Heat stress is caused by an imbalance in transpiration, the loss of water vapor from the plant.

DAMAGE
In hot weather, water evaporates from plants' leaves faster than it can be taken up by the roots. As a result, the plant becomes dehydrated. Signs include yellow leaves, wilted foliage, and shriveled pseudobulbs. Pseudobulbs store water and nutrients. They shrivel when their resources are depleted. If a heat-stressed orchid has leaves that are not merely wilted but hard and leathery, you may not be able to save the plant.

PREVENTION AND MANAGEMENT
To prevent heat stress, raise humidity with dry wells and humidity trays or a misting system. Improve air circulation with a small fan and adequate space between potted plants. Watering won't help because roots can absorb only so much water. Move the orchid to a shady spot. Some orchids are more heat-tolerant than others. Many vandas are happy in 90°F weather and require high heat to bloom. Most cymbidiums, on the other hand, will refuse to flower when temperatures rise above 80°F.

Sunburn
The sun can burn orchid leaves if they're placed in an inappropriate exposure unless the plants are properly acclimated to outdoor light.

DAMAGE
Initial signs of sunburn are red or purple pigmentation on orchid foliage, either in spots or throughout the leaf. This pigmentation is a protective reaction most common in drought-tolerant, thick-leaved orchids. Foliage returns to its original color once overexposure is corrected. Delicate orchids with thin leaves may scorch in response to overly bright sunlight. The brown or tan spots won't ever regreen and should be trimmed to improve the appearance of the plant. Other symptoms of sunburn include bud blast, premature flower dropping, and flower spikes that fail to develop buds.

PREVENTION AND MANAGEMENT
Sunburn is easy to avoid. If you've moved your orchids outdoors for the summer, follow the instructions in Chapter 4 for acclimating your orchids to the outdoor light. If you grow on a windowsill or in a greenhouse, remember that summer sun is brighter (at a more obtuse angle from sun to Earth) and warmer than winter sun. Use shade cloth or a sheer curtain to protect your plants.

Drought damage
Prolonged drought can kill an orchid in two ways. It can cause roots to shrivel and die, which prevents the absorption of nutrients. It also can desiccate leaf tissue, killing chlorophyll and making photosynthesis impossible.

DAMAGE
Pleated foliage is a classic sign. It affects thin-leaved orchids such as cymbidiums, oncidiums, miltonias, and zygopetalums. Pleated foliage never straightens out, but if you increase the watering frequency, future foliage should grow in straight. Prune the distorted leaf if you dislike how it looks, but it won't hurt the plant if you leave it. Thick-leaved orchids such as phalaenopsis, cattleyas, dendrobiums, and vandas become leathery when drought-stressed. The leaf's surface looks puckered and takes on the texture of a tanned hide. Other signs of underwatering include shriveled pseudobulbs, bud blast, and loss of vigor. These problems have a long-lasting effect on your plant.

PREVENTION AND MANAGEMENT
Depending on how soon you recognize the problem, you may be able to rehydrate the damaged leaves by moving plants to a highly humid location and changing your watering routine. If the foliage does not plump up, cut off the disfigured leaves.

Rot & overwatering
It is all too easy to kill an orchid by overwatering. Most orchid roots grow best if they're not surrounded by a heavy, wet potting mix. A fast-draining, porous bark mix decreases the chances of root rot and death by overwatering, but it's still possible.

DAMAGE
When an orchid is overwatered, it's not a question of delivering too much water at once, it's a question of watering an orchid too frequently and not allowing it to dry out between waterings. If the velamen on epiphytic orchid roots doesn't dry out between waterings, it rots and disintegrates. Without velamen, the root can't absorb water or nutrients, and the orchid dies. Orchids weakened by overwatering and subsequent (but not complete) root loss are more vulnerable to pathogens.

PREVENTION AND MANAGEMENT
If your orchids are potted in plastic or other nonporous materials, check your mix before watering. Even bark mix can stay wet in a nonporous container. For orchids potted in long-grain sphagnum moss, poke a finger into the moss at least an inch or two to make sure watering is necessary.

Nutritional issues
Many people overfeed their orchids. While it is possible for an orchid to suffer from nutrient deficiency (yellowing leaves may signal lack of nitrogen), it is more common to overfeed an orchid.

DAMAGE
Dark green foliage is often a sign of too much nitrogen, which usually causes reduced flowering. Brown leaf tips may indicate too much fertilizer in the root zone. Overfertilization can burn (dry out) plant roots, killing them and making it impossible for the orchid to absorb water and nutrients. Most fertilizer material is composed of a chemical salt. Water moves through plant tissue from areas of low salt to areas of high salt concentration. As plants lose water via transpiration, the salt concentration inside plant tissue rises, and more water is absorbed (if available) from surrounding soil or potting mix. If plants are overfertilized, the salt concentration in the potting mix surrounding their roots is raised, which can draw water out of the plant.

PREVENTION AND MANAGEMENT
If you see signs of fertilizer burn, remove as much potting mix as possible from the roots. Soak the root ball in water for 5 to 10 minutes, then repot in fresh bark mix and correct your fertilization routine.

Creating an orchid hospital

? ASK THE GARDEN DOCTOR

Can orchids make my pets sick?

ANSWER: Probably not, unless the orchids have been sprayed with a toxic pesticide. Indoor cats often chew on monocot leaves to stimulate regurgitation, and orchids are monocots. Thin-leaved orchids are most appealing, so if your cat is a chewer, place them out of reach.

As hard as you try to keep your orchids healthy, there will

be times when one or more needs special care. It's important to create an intensive care unit where you can tend to problem plants without fear of contaminating their neighbors.

If you can set up an orchid hospital in a separate room, great. If not, at least provide a separate windowsill or growing area 10 or 15 feet away from the rest of your collection.

What an orchid hospital does

The ICU should offer medium warmth and bright, indirect light (recuperating orchids are stressed by direct sun and temperature extremes). You should be able to set up a small fan in case you need to increase air circulation for orchids recovering from fungal or bacterial diseases.

You should also find a way to increase humidity in the area—perhaps with a mini greenhouse or humidity tent—to help orchids rehydrate from the beginning stages of drought stress.

Pest-disease triangle

When considering orchid health, learn about the pest-disease triangle. Three elements are

necessary for a pathogen to successfully attack any plant. If you eliminate one of those three variables, you'll eliminate the pathogen problem.

First, consider the pathogen itself. Can you keep your collection free of bacteria, fungi, insects, mites, and so forth? It's not always possible to completely eliminate pathogens, but you should be able to limit them through vigilance and good cultural practices.

Second, consider the plants. Certain pathogens are host-specific. For example, since black rot is most prevalent among cattleya orchids, if you don't grow cattleyas, your orchids may never have black spot.

Third, look at the environment. By correctly controlling temperature, humidity, and water you can make growing conditions inhospitable to pests and diseases. If a black spot spore lands in your living room but finds no standing water, it will die without causing damage.

When to turn off life support

Sadly, there are times when the merciful thing to do is pull the plug. If disease or pest predation isn't caught early, you run the risk of infecting the rest of your orchids. Sometimes, even if the plant can be cured, it is so disfigured that it will never be beautiful again.

Unless this plant has great sentimental value, it's best to throw it away. By no means should it go in the compost pile, where pests and disease pathogens might live on to infect other plants.

Opposite: **Look for inexpensive mini greenhouses at hardware or big-box stores, or make your own with shelves and plastic, to house orchids that need special treatment.**

Above left: **The shriveled leaves of this miniature phalaenopsis indicate it is stressed.**

Above right: **Ten days after removing the sphagnum moss, repotting the orchid in fresh bark mix, and keeping it under a bell jar to add humidity, the same phalaenopsis is on the road to recovery.**

special projects

Once you've successfully grown a few orchids, you may want to flex your muscles with some special projects to customize your collection.

p.110
CREATE BARK MIXES

You can nab premade bark mixes off the garden center shelf, but once you understand the kinds of orchids you grow, you may want to blend your own.

p.114
SPECIAL DISPLAYS

Orchids grow on bark or cork slabs, on tree branches, or in slatted baskets. They're easier projects than you might think.

p.120
ORCHID PARTNERS

Orchids love to grow with plant companions. Find out which houseplants go best with the orchids you grow.

p.124
ADDING LIGHT

Even if you live in a dark basement apartment, you can grow orchids by adding the right kind of light.

p.128
GROWING IN TERRARIUMS

Orchids like extra humidity, and they look nifty under glass. Find out why a terrarium can be an orchid's best friend.

Create bark mixes

Why would you want to make your own bark mix when you can buy a perfectly good bag of orchid mix at any garden center?

Well, why would you want to bake a cake when you can pick one up at a grocery store? Because not only is homemade sometimes better, it's fun making something from scratch.

Commercially available bark mixes are usually medium grain, appropriate for most epiphytes. Their primary ingredient is fir bark (that's not the same as pine bark) and they also contain one or more of the following: perlite, vermiculite, peat moss, long-grain sphagnum moss, coir, fern fiber, and charcoal.

There are as many recipes for bark mix as there are for barbecue, and as you sample different varieties, you'll find the one that's best for you and your orchids.

Bark offers air circulation
Look for a mix that offers good aeration by providing substantial particles and equally large air spaces. A good rule: the thicker an orchid's roots, the coarser the bark it needs.

For most orchids, this means a medium-grain fir bark with individual pieces that are approximately ½ inch in diameter.

Fine-grain mixes (sometimes called seedling mixes) with bark pieces approximately ¼ inch in diameter are better for orchids that require more moisture, such as miltonias, paphiopedilums, and phragmipediums.

Coarse-grain bark has pieces about 1 inch in diameter and is appropriate for some of the large cattleyas.

Other ingredients
Once you've decided whether you need a fine-, medium-, or coarse-grain mix, consider the ingredients. Think about your personal approach to orchid care to help you choose.

For example, some orchid mixes contain small ceramic balls like those used in hydroponic growing. These ceramic pieces provide fast drainage and do not biodegrade, extending the useful lifetime of a mix. If you're growing drought-tolerant epiphytes and fear you might overwater, or if you'd like to put off repotting as

Above: **Phalaenopsis orchids grow best in a medium-grain bark mix that provides good drainage.**

long as possible, a mix with ceramic pieces may be perfect for you and your plants.

If, on the other hand, you tend to underwater, or you travel frequently and can only care for your orchids at weekly intervals, look for a mix with long-grain sphagnum moss.

This type of moss holds moisture longer than other orchid mix components. When used in conjunction with other ingredients, it is less prone to overwatering than when used alone. (See Chapter 4.)

Hydrate mix first

Before you use any mix, be sure it's fully hydrated. Estimate how much mix you'll need for your repotting project, pour it into a watertight bucket, then fill the bucket with warm water and let it sit for 8 to 10 hours.

The next day, strain the excess water from the mix. This allows each particle to absorb as much moisture as possible and removes dust.

Avoid mixes with fertilizer

Some orchid mixes come with fertilizer already added, which isn't necessarily a good thing. It's hard to keep track of a fertilization routine if you don't know exactly what is being delivered and when.

For example, one brand of orchid mix includes a time-release fertilizer with an NPK (nitrogen, phosphorus, and potassium) ratio of .1–.02–.05.

The first reason not to use it is that it contains a tiny amount of fertilizer. Second, it contains five times as much nitrogen as phosphorus—feeding foliage at the expense of flowers. Third, time-release fertilizers work poorly with bark mixes.

You're better off feeding your orchids exactly what they need, when they need it. Many orchids bloom without fertilizer, just as they do in nature.

What about those packing peanuts?

Have you ever knocked an orchid out of its pot only to be surprised by a layer of polystyrene peanuts in the bottom?

Because of its low cost and extreme light weight, polystyrene is a popular potting material with commercial growers who save money on shipping and potting mix. However, since it provides no nutrition and retains no moisture (and looks less than beautiful), polystyrene should be used only in small quantities.

If you have a deep pot and the entire volume is not required to accommodate the roots of your orchid, it's fine to add a few peanuts to the bottom to keep it lightweight.

Avoid reducing the amount of organic potting mix you're using. The polystyrene should be a minor addition, not a substitute for any organic component.

TEST GARDEN TIP

If you don't mix your own

Fafard makes an excellent orchid potting mix containing fir bark, large perlite particles, and both coir chips and coir fiber. If you buy a ready-made mix, it's worth paying a little extra for a quality product. It's available at independent nurseries and garden centers.

Left: **Four parts fir bark to one part perlite and one part horticultural charcoal is a medium-grain recipe.**

Above: **The same ingredients, blended. When potting orchids, be sure to dip deep into the bag or bowl, because the perlite and charcoal tend to sink to the bottom.**

Make a custom bark mix

Choose the ingredients best for your orchids and the way you grow them.

Start by mixing a small batch and seeing how it works with a few plants before going on a repotting spree. You may decide to tweak your recipe as you learn more about how it behaves over time.

To experiment with additional components, begin by adding one part of any additional ingredient at a time so you can monitor how it affects orchid growth and maintenance.

It's generally a poor idea to reuse orchid mix. Fresh mix is not only sterile and pathogen-free, but it also has the structural integrity necessary for good drainage.

Old mix has already begun to break down and will not drain as quickly as fresh mix. It might also contain bacteria or fungi.

The following page describes many of the major components used in orchid mixes.

Above: **The potting mix you use for a phalaenopsis orchid depends on your watering schedule. Use a medium-grain mix and water more frequently or a fine-grain mix and water less often.**

CHARCOAL

Horticultural charcoal is hardwood charcoal (not compressed briquettes) added to "sweeten" bark mixes. That means the charcoal absorbs and neutralizes acids and bacteria that can accumulate in decomposing organic mixes. Charcoal doesn't retain water or contribute nutrition to the orchid mix.

COIR AND COCONUT PALM

Coir, a fiber extracted from the husks of coconut shells, can substitute for long-grain sphagnum moss. Coconut husk chunks are also called coir chunks. A substitute for fir bark, they are more water-retentive. Ground coconut husks may substitute for peat moss. Wash or soak thoroughly before using to remove excess salt.

FERN FIBERS

Fern fibers are taken from the stems of tropical tree ferns and osmunda ferns but neither is harvested sustainably. While both osmunda and tree fern fibers come from ferns, they are two separate things; the terms are not interchangeable. Fern fibers in slab form are sometimes used to mount orchids.

FIR BARK

Bark from the Douglas fir is an organic material sold in three grades or sizes: fine, medium, and coarse. Fir bark is inexpensive, renewable, and easy to find. Epiphytic orchids that grow on bark in nature adapt well. Fir bark is water-retentive and provides nutrition as it biodegrades in one to two years, depending on the grade.

PEAT MOSS

Like perlite and vermiculite, peat moss provides no nutrition but is highly absorbent and sterile. Peat is dead, decomposed sphagnum moss. Because it takes hundreds of years to form in bogs, new peat cannot be created at the same rate at which peat is harvested. Many growers avoid using it.

PERLITE

Perlite is volcanic ash that has been expanded through heat treatment. It is inexpensive and lightweight, provides no nutrition, decomposes slowly, and retains some water. Coarse-grade perlite is better suited to orchid mix than finer, horticultural-grade perlite.

SPHAGNUM MOSS

Long-grain sphagnum moss can hold many times its weight in water, making it useful in bark mixes, which generally drain fast. Sphagnum moss regrows quickly after harvest and is not endangered. However, it is difficult to rewet if allowed to dry out entirely, and remains wet at its interior while deceptively dry on its surface.

VERMICULITE

Vermiculite is expanded mica. It is light and porous, decomposes slowly, and retains both water and nutrition (from fertilizer solution). Vermiculite is often confused with perlite, but looks quite different. Perlite is white, while vermiculite is light brown or tan and sometimes shiny. It retains more moisture than perlite.

Custom bark mix recipes Here are two basic recipes to get you started.

RECIPE FOR YOUNG PLANTS

This fine-grade orchid mix is good for young offshoots and fine-root terrestrial orchids:
4 parts fine-grade
  fir bark
1 part long-grain
  sphagnum moss
1 part horticultural
  charcoal
1 part perlite or
  vermiculite

RECIPE FOR TREE-GROWING ORCHIDS

This medium-grade mix is appropriate for most epiphytes:
4 parts medium-grade
  fir bark
1 part horticultural
  charcoal
1 part perlite or
  vermiculite

Placing orchids on slabs

A tree fern fiber slab serves as the mounting base for a *Dendrobium aggregatum*, allowing its yellow bloom spikes to cascade downward.

Once you've mastered a DIY bark mix, consider placing an orchid on a slab. Epiphytes and lithophytes can be grown mounted on tree fern fiber or cork bark. It's close to how these orchids grow in nature and guarantees excellent drainage for velamen roots.

Some orchids, such as vandas and some cattleya members, truly thrive only when mounted. Even the quick drainage of a coarse-grain bark mix allows too much moisture to surround their roots.

While orchids displayed in this manner require watering and feeding more often than orchids in pots, their care is not more complicated.

Mounting an orchid is simple and a fun project for anyone who likes crafts. Hang your finished project in a nook such as a bay window or in a high-humidity area such as a bathroom.

Cork bark slabs

To begin, fasten a U-shape staple to the top of a cork bark slab. This will be the hanger once the orchid is in place. You should be able to tap it in gently with a hammer. For extra security, dab a bead of glue at each entry point.

Lay the slab flat and observe its topography. Cork bark has hollows where orchid roots fit naturally. Find the best spot and place the orchid in this hollow.

There are two ways to attach the orchid to the slab: with hot glue or fishing line. If you are using hot glue, start by marking where two or three points of the plant come in contact with the bark. These contact points should be low on the pseudobulbs and canes, not the roots. If only the roots are glued into place, the weight of the top growth may pull the orchid off its mount.

Using a glue gun on the lowest setting (a high setting would damage plant tissue), dab the glue onto the cork and the marked contact points. The glue dries rapidly, so move quickly. Gently press the orchid onto the bark, making sure each of the contact points is met. Allow the glue to dry for several hours, then soak the slab in a basin of water for 10 to 15 minutes and allow excess water to drain before hanging the orchid.

Over the next several months, the orchid's roots will grow onto the cork bark, holding it firmly in place. By the time the glue dissolves (after 6 to 12 months, depending on water and humidity levels) it will no longer be needed.

If the plant is in active growth or in a high-light, high-heat situation, it could need water every day. If it's dormant, it may need water only every five days or even less often.

Water as needed by soaking the slab in water for 10 to 15 minutes.

If you are using fishing line to attach the orchid to the bark, follow the following instructions for the fern fiber slabs.

Fern fiber slabs

If you have selected fern fiber, begin by attaching a U-shape staple to the top. Since a fern fiber slab is flat and full of large air spaces, glue is less effective as a mounting method.

Instead, place a small clump of long-grain sphagnum moss in the center of the bottom third of the slab. The clump should be about the same size as the root ball of the orchid being mounted.

Place the orchid roots on top of the moss, leaving room for the roots to grow down and foliage and stems to grow up. Place another small clump of moss on top of the orchid roots,

then use the monofilament to tie the orchid in place, crisscrossing the root ball front and back at least twice.

The moss prevents plant tissue from being cut by the monofilament and also retains some moisture against the roots. You could also use a length of nylon pantyhose to tie the orchid in place instead of using the protective moss. Most people find the monofilament more aesthetically pleasing since it's almost invisible.

Soak the slab in a basin of water for 10 to 15 minutes and allow it to drain before hanging your orchid in place. To water the slab, soak it in water for 10 to 15 minutes, following the guidelines for the cork bark slab on frequency.

After several months, check the roots of your plant. You'll see that they have grown into the fern fiber. At this point, you can remove the monofilament or pantyhose.

Growing orchids on a slab

Orchids can grow on slabs, including cork bark or fern fiber, available from orchid nurseries and garden centers, and online. If you use bark, you can can attach the orchid with glue from a glue gun on a low temperature setting. However, fern fiber slabs are too porous to use glue. Fishing line may be an easier option, and it works with both bark and fern fiber. Eventually, the orchid's roots will grow right onto the slab, allowing you to remove the fishing line or other flexible supports (such as slender strips of pantyhose) that held it there originally.

MATERIALS LIST

Epiphytic or lithophytic orchid
  such as vanda, cattleya,
  dendrobium, phalaenopsis
Cork bark or tree fern fiber slabs
Hot-glue gun (for bark only)
Glue sticks
Transparent monofilament
  fishing line
Scissors (if using fishing line)
Pantyhose (optional)
Long-grain sphagnum moss
1-inch U-shape staple

1 POSITION
Place a bit of moistened sphagnum moss on the slab where the orchid's roots will grow, and position the orchid where you want it.

2 WRAP
Add more moist sphagnum moss on top of the orchid's roots, then wrap fishing line gently around the slab until the orchid is secure.

3 WATER
Soak the entire slab in water for 10 to 15 minutes every few days, depending on the growth cycle of the orchid. A sink or large basin is ideal.

4 HANG
Because the slab may be wet, it's good to hang it on a surface that can handle moisture or suspend it on a hook in a bay window or other open nook.

Creating an orchid tree

Expand your vision by working on a larger scale.

Instead of a single specimen, you can create a hanging or freestanding multi-orchid display by grouping several epiphytes on a branch or log.

First, consider where you want to place your finished project, so you can choose a branch of the appropriate size. You'll need to decide whether it will be hung or freestanding. Look around outdoors for a solid branch with an interesting shape and some indentations or forks where you can place your plants.

Prune off any unwanted pieces, scrub the branch with a 10 percent bleach solution, then let it dry.

Drought-tolerant orchids with succulent foliage, such as phalaenopsis, cattleyas, vandas, dendrobiums, and oncidiums, are best suited to this project. Avoid those that need constant moisture, such as paphiopedilums, phragmipediums, and miltonias, or any that are large and heavy, such as cymbidiums.

How to display an orchid tree

A hanging branch looks dramatic in a large window or against a solid-color wall. Screw stainless-steel eyes into the back or top of the branch, then apply a dab of glue to cement them in place. These eyes can be hung from hooks screwed into the wall or window frame, or strung with a thin cable.

A freestanding branch "tree" gives you more flexibility of placement should you want to rearrange your interior landscape. For this, a clay pot makes an excellent base. The weight of the pot helps keep the branch upright, and the terra-cotta blends in well with the rest of your potted plants.

Begin by placing a drop cloth over your working area.

Position the branch in the pot and add stones around the base of the branch for ballast and to help keep the branch in position.

Cover the pot's drainage hole. Pour Quikrete or plaster of Paris into the pot, firming it around the base of the branch. Although both of these

Left: **The finished orchid tree includes two miniature phalaenopsis, a small oncidium, and a variegated vanilla. The spiky tillandsia (air plant) at the base adds another texture.**

materials' surfaces dry in 20 to 30 minutes, let them sit overnight before the next step.

Arranging orchids on a branch

Before you begin, think about possible orchid placement. Hold the plants up against the branch to get an idea of how they'll look. It's better to experiment now than when the orchids' roots are bare and vulnerable.

The branch will look better if you limit the project to three or four different types of orchids to avoid having them compete for attention. Choose colors and types that work together as a cohesive unit.

How to attach the orchids

Assemble your tools: scissors, sphagnum moss, and transparent fishing line. Choose the focal point of the branch and start there, working outward. Generally it's best to start with the largest orchid, using smaller plants to fill in the gaps as you go. Remove the first orchid from its pot and shake off as much potting mix as possible.

Wrap the roots in moss and tie the roots in their moss bundle to the tree. It's similar to tying a single orchid to a fern fiber slab. Pause as you work and look at the branch from every angle. If it has small side twigs, you may be able to tuck a moss-and-root bundle into a natural niche without any tying at all.

After about six months, you should be able to remove the fishing line as the orchids' roots grow onto the branch.

You can use hot glue to affix your orchids to the branch, but it's better to use sphagnum moss and fishing line. The extra moisture held by the sphagnum moss is a bonus because large planted branches are more cumbersome to water than small mounted orchids.

Water and fertilize

You'll probably need to water the orchids on your branch once or twice a week. Take it to a sink or shower, depending on its size. Give it a good drenching, let it sit for 15 to 20 minutes, then drench it again.

To fertilize, you'll need to spray a foliar feed. Any mounted orchid, whether a single specimen or a planted branch, requires more frequent attention since it's not growing in a mix that retains water and nutrients.

ASK THE GARDEN DOCTOR

What plants partner with orchid trees?

ANSWER: You can add epiphytic houseplants to an orchid tree. Hoyas, philodendrons, and creeping figs are vines that adapt well to branch culture. Several weeks after mounting, their roots attach to the wood's surface, and the plants cover the branch with foliage, providing a lush backdrop for orchid blooms.

How to make an orchid tree
Orchids grow wild on trees. You can play Mother Nature by creating a branch planted in a pot or to hang in your home.

1 GATHER
Place all your materials on a drop cloth to make the process smoother and easier to clean up. If you're placing the branch in a pot, set it in plaster of Paris or Quikrete the night before.

2 PLACE
Wrap bundles of moist sphagnum moss around the roots of your orchids. The moss keeps the roots hydrated while they grow onto the branch or log.

3 ATTACH
Cut a short length of transparent fishing line with scissors, then wrap the line around the moss bundle until it is securely attached to the branch.

MATERIALS LIST
Drought-tolerant orchids with succulent foliage, such as phalaenopsis, cattleyas, vandas, dendrobiums, oncidiums
Drop cloth
Scissors
Branch or log cleaned with a 10 percent bleach and 90 percent water solution
Transparent monofilament fishing line
Long-grain sphagnum moss
Large pot (optional)
Quikrete or plaster of Paris (if planting in a pot)
Other plants, such as tillandsias, to fill in the base

Planting an orchid basket

An orchid basket does not always need to hang, but orchids in baskets need good air circulation.

Transplanting an orchid from a traditional pot

to a slatted hanging basket (also called a box) is a simple process. Many epiphytes, including all vandas, grow better this way. If you tend to be overly generous with watering, growing an orchid in a box may keep it from rotting.

How to plant

Remove the orchid from its pot and shake off as much of the potting mix as possible. Choose a wooden basket barely large enough to accommodate the root ball. A tight fit ensures secure placement.

Line the box with a piece of sheet moss to keep the potting medium from washing out through the slats. Sheet moss is not the same as long-grain sphagnum moss. It is *Hypnum curvifolium*, a moss that grows in large, carpetlike mats on the forest floor.

If you can't find sheet moss, you can use coir, like the type used for hanging baskets, but rinse it thoroughly first because it can hold salt.

Sprinkle a thin layer of bark mix over the moss at the bottom of the basket. While vandaceous orchids don't actually require potting mix in their baskets, the addition of a little mix improves moisture retention and anchorage while the orchids' roots take hold.

Place the orchid in the center of the basket if it's monopodial and with its oldest growth against the side of the basket if it's sympodial.

While holding the orchid in place with one hand, pour small amounts of bark mix around the edges, gently poking it under and around the roots until the orchid can stand on its own and the orchid is replanted at its original level.

Watering an orchid box

Soak everything in a shallow bowl for 10 to 15 minutes so both the wooden box and the potting medium get thoroughly wet.

Be sure to let everything drain thoroughly before hanging the box. Since this orchid won't have an attached saucer, getting rid of the excess water before hanging the box in place is especially important.

TEST GARDEN TIP

Watering an orchid basket

A box or basket made from slats of wood provides excellent contact between orchid roots and the surrounding air, which is how most epiphytes grow in nature. An orchid potted in a basket or box will require more frequent watering than the same plant growing in a pot. You might even have to water it every day. If you're growing in the high humidity of the tropics or in a greenhouse, the moisture from the air can be absorbed directly by the orchid's roots.

How to plant an orchid basket

Orchids with roots that need extra air circulation, including vandas, prefer to grow in a slatted basket.

MATERIALS LIST

An epiphytic orchid such as a vanda
A slatted wooden basket, available from garden centers or online
Sheet moss (*Hypnum curvifolium*)
Coarse- or medium-grain bark mix
Transparent monofilament fishing line
Hangers for the basket

1 PLANT
Select a container just slightly larger than the roots of your orchid. Line the basket with sheet moss, then add just a bit of bark mix to help hold the roots in place.

2 HANG
Place the basket in a location where the orchid will get plenty of light and air. To water, soak the basket for 10 to 15 minutes, but remember to let it drain thoroughly before rehanging.

Orchid partners

You already know that
grouping plants together raises ambient humidity, which is a good thing. Creating an interior landscape, rather than just lining up your orchids in a neat row, also increases the visual impact of your indoor garden.

A bright window with a built-in bay or a large sill is a perfect place to start. If you have a radiator underneath the sill, be careful. Add a layer of insulation to protect orchids from too much bottom heat. Increased temperatures also dry the air, so add a dry well or orchid tray.

Vary your landscape
Create levels by combining hanging baskets with potted orchids. If you can't hang a basket, use plant stands, shelving, and upside-down pots to lift some orchids higher than others. If you have a potted tree such as a ficus (fig) or a palm, hang mounted orchids from the branches and let your epiphytes be epiphytes.

Group orchids according to their needs. In other words, avoid placing a sun-loving cattleya next to a shade-needing paphiopedilum.

In nature, orchids grow in concert with other tropical plants, and you can do this indoors as well. The juxtaposition of colors, shapes, and textures gives your interior landscape a depth and complexity that comes only from diversity. By choosing companion plants for your orchids you can create your own tropical tableau.

Above: **A sunny bay window is an ideal location for medium-light partners such as phalaenopsis with lipstick plant and stephanotis. A temperature and humidity gauge helps monitor conditions.**

HIGH-LIGHT PARTNERS FOR: Aerangis, angraecum, ascocenda, ascocentrum, catasetum, cattleya, cycnoches, cycnodes, cymbidium, dendrobium, oncidium, pleione, rhynchostylis, rhynchovanda, vanda

CROTON (*Codiaeum variegatum*) The variegated foliage of this tropical plant provides year-round interest. Even when no orchids are blooming, there's something colorful to admire. Leaves are marked with yellow, orange, red, and/or white, and older plants develop a woody stem. Crotons can grow to tree height or be pruned to stay smaller.

KUMQUAT (*Fortunella margarita*) Kumquat is one of the easiest citruses to grow indoors because it requires less intense sunlight and produces smaller fruit. The fragrant white flowers produce ornamental bright orange fruits about the size of a quail's egg. The tree's woody structure can be used as a rack on which to hang small mounted orchids. The leaves create a canopy, so orchids hung below receive less light than the tree.

MANDEVILLA VINE (*Mandevilla × amabilis*) Train this vine around a window frame to define the boundaries of your display or grow it on a pyramid for vertical interest. Glossy foliage stays attractive year-round, and the white, pink, or magenta flowers are prolific during summer.

STEPHANOTIS (*Stephanotis floribunda*) Use this vine like a mandevilla. It's also sometimes called Madagascar jasmine. When given enough light, it produces white fragrant flowers year-round.

MEDIUM-LIGHT PARTNERS FOR: Aerangis, angraecum, ascocenda, ascocentrum, catasetum, cattleya, coelogyne, cycnoches, cycnodes, dendrobium, dendrochilum, doritaenopsis, doritis, gongora, haraella, masdevallia, neofinitia, oncidium, phalaenopsis, phragmipedium, pleione, pleurothallis, rhynchostylis

AIR PLANT (*Tillandsia capitata*) The diminutive epiphyte is round and portable. It can be tucked into the forks of tree branches, mounted with hot glue to a display branch, or simply placed on the bark mix at the base of an orchid, posing as a groundcover. Almost any air plant can be used this way.

LIPSTICK PLANT (*Aeschynanthus marmoratus*) Lipstick plant provides a dense cascade of green leaves that may be marbled with red and yellow. Some lipstick plant species have bright red or orange flowers and plain, dark green foliage. Choose the one you like best.

MISTLETOE CACTUS (*Rhipsalis baccifera*) This epiphytic cactus adds great texture with slim, leafless, vertical stems. Potted or mounted on a branch as part of an epiphytic display, it should be allowed to hang for best effect. Other species of *Rhipsalis* also work well.

WAX PLANT (*Hoya carnosa*) A low-maintenance vine with succulent green to green-and-white leaves, wax plant may be trained around a window frame or displayed in a hanging basket. It produces umbels of small pale pink flowers. *H. carnosa rubra*, with red stems, is pictured. Other species of hoya are suited to medium-light locations, but *H. carnosa* is easy to find. It grows well in an east or west window and likes to dry out between waterings.

LOW-LIGHT PARTNERS FOR: Doritaenopsis, doritis, jewel orchids, masdevallia, paphiopedilum, phalaenopsis, pleurothallis

CREEPING FIG (*Ficus pumila*) This tropical groundcover grows in both low and medium light. Its dime-size leaves are medium green and strongly textured. The stem will root in high humidity where it comes in contact with the ground or wall or tree bark. Use creeping fig as a trailing houseplant or let it climb up a trellis. It can also be used to fill in empty spaces on a planted orchid branch.

GRAPE IVY (*Cissus rhombifolia*) This sprawling vine can easily fill a large bay window with greenery, either hanging from above or sitting on a windowsill and trained up and around. Its jointed stems are a fuzzy, tawny reddish-brown.

RABBIT'S FOOT FERN (*Polypodium aureum*) Ferns and orchids are natural companions, creating a mini rain forest on a windowsill. Rabbit's foot fern is a low-maintenance plant with tall, (24- to 36-inch), upright, light green fronds and fuzzy rhizomes that creep along the soil's surface.

STAGHORN FERN (*Platycerium bifurcatum*) A large, architectural plant, staghorn fern has gray-green foliage covered with white fuzz. Fronds grow up and out, vertically and horizontally, as long as 24 to 36 inches. Staghorn fern can be placed in a hanging basket, a standard pot, or grown as a mounted specimen.

Adding light

Not everyone is fortunate enough to have a home full of large bay windows just waiting to be filled with orchids. If you have no natural light or not enough to grow what you want, you can supplement with artificial light.

Various kinds of bulbs give off different colors and intensities of light. You have many choices, depending on what you want to grow and what kind of light fixtures you have.

Regular incandescent or halogen light bulbs should never be considered appropriate grow lights. While the light is pleasant to the human eye, it isn't right for plant growth, and the bulbs give off so much heat that you risk burning plant tissue if the light is placed too close to the orchid.

Characteristics of light

There are three characteristics of light to consider when you're deciding which type of bulb to use: color, intensity, and duration.

Above: **If you're growing orchids in a room with little or no natural light, consider buying a plant stand with built-in grow lights.**

Color: While the sun emits light in all colors of the visible spectrum, light in the blue and red ranges is most important for plant growth. Orchids (and all flowering plants) require large amounts of orange-red light in order to bloom, and blue light promotes lush, compact foliage growth.

Intensity: Light intensity is measured in foot-candles, which is defined as the strength of light given off by one candle at a distance of one foot. (See Chapter 3). Light intensity is the single most important factor in photosynthesis. Less-than-optimum light intensity may not kill a plant, but can result in leggy, weak growth or decreased flowering and fruiting. Consider that outdoors on a sunny day, light intensity measures approximately 10,000 foot-candles. A sunny indoor room has much less intense light, about 3,500 foot-candles.

Duration: Since artificial light doesn't exactly duplicate the intensity of sunlight, you can compensate by giving plants more hours of artificial light than they would receive in their native habitats. Increased quantity compensates for reduced quality.

Scientists once believed that plants require a period of darkness to metabolize the food they made during photosynthesis, so grow lights were not allowed to run around the clock. Research now shows that darkness may not be required for metabolism after all, which means a rest period may not be necessary for all plants. Once called the dark reaction, the metabolic process has been renamed the light-independent reaction.

How bright should it be?

What's bright to you may not be bright to a plant. Household bulbs don't give off enough energy in the right parts of the spectrum to be useful for plant growth. When you're evaluating the available light, turn off all the lamps in a room and judge based on natural light. Supplement with special grow bulbs to increase light levels for optimum orchid growth.

ASK THE GARDEN DOCTOR

Is a table lamp good for orchids?

ANSWER: No. Regular incandescent or halogen bulbs don't emit the right type of light for growing any houseplants, including orchids. Plus, you risk burning plants if you place them close to the heated bulbs.

Left: **Fluorescent bulbs can be used for growing orchids. Choose the light most appealing to you since both cool and warm bulbs are useful for plant growth.**

Types of bulbs

The brightest bulbs are high intensity discharge (HID) lights. They can be installed in your home, garage, or greenhouse to supplement or serve as the sole source of light for your plants. HID bulbs pass electricity through a glass or ceramic tube containing a mixture of gases. The blend of gases determines the color of the light given off by each type of lamp. All HID lights run from regular 120-volt household current, but they require special fixtures with ballasts.

There are two types of HID bulbs: metal halide (MH) and high-pressure sodium (HPS). Both emit more intense light than fluorescent lamps. HID lights are twice as efficient as fluorescent: one 400-watt halide lamp emits as much light as 800 watts of fluorescent tubes.

Using both bulbs together

You can use MH and HPS bulbs in a single location, but a metal halide bulb cannot be used in a high-pressure sodium fixture and vice versa. (HPS ballasts include an igniter; MH ballasts do not.) If you use multiple fixtures, consider combining HPS and MH systems. With only one fixture, try a conversion bulb that uses metal halide to promote foliage growth and a high-pressure sodium bulb to encourage flowering.

How much wattage do you need?

When choosing the wattage of HID lamps, determine how much space you need to illuminate. As a rule, you want 20 to 40 watts per square foot of garden. Divide the wattage of your bulb by 20 (for example, 1,000 divided by 20 equals 50), then divide the wattage of your bulb by 40 (1,000 divided by 40 equals 25). This gives you the outer limits of the light intensity range.

With one 1,000-watt system, you can light between 25 and 50 square feet of interior landscape. Adjust your setup as you observe how well your plants grow. Increase or decrease the intensity of the light accordingly by shifting the placement of your plants or the light fixture, but not by changing the bulb in the lamp to one with more watts. Each lamp is designed for a specific wattage, and a 400-watt bulb cannot operate safely in a 250-watt system.

Fluorescent tubes

High-intensity fluorescent bulbs are also an excellent choice. Cool and warm bulbs are available. Choose the light most appealing to you since both are useful for plant growth.

Above: **Strong natural light and fluorescent tubes are a good combination for medium-light orchids.**

Right: **A clip-on appliance made by Agrosun provides a targeted amount of light.**

Traditional fluorescent tubes, in inexpensive shop light fixtures or on multitiered grow stations, are the most economical. Fluorescent tubes produce considerably less intense light than HID or high-intensity fluorescent bulbs. If you're only supplementing natural light, fluorescent tubes may work well.

The ends of fluorescent tubes emit less light than the center. Place lower-light plants under or near the ends. Replace the tubes every 18 months if they are being used approximately 16 hours per day.

How high should my bulbs be?

Light is hot, and some lights emit more heat than others. HID lights emit the most heat. Depending on the wattage, bulbs should be positioned 2 to 6 feet above plant foliage.

High-output fluorescent bulbs can be 2 to 4 feet above plants. Traditional fluorescent tubes are the coolest. You can use them a mere 6 inches from foliage without burning plant tissue.

Increased heat leads to decreased humidity and faster drying of potting medium, so plants under lights need more frequent watering.

ASK THE GARDEN DOCTOR

Should I use LED lights to grow orchids?

ANSWER: LED lights are not well-suited to home orchid growing. The lights are expensive, and the color of the light they produce is strongly pink or blue. Neither is attractive for in-home orchid growing.

Left: **Indoor lighting is a substitute for outdoor light. Orchids grown outdoors in shade receive more light than those grown indoors with bulbs.**

Types of bulbs
The type of light you choose depends on what kind of orchid you're growing and where you're growing it.

FLUORESCENT LIGHTS
Bulbs are cool, warm, or full spectrum. Light from cool tubes has a blue cast to it, while warm tubes emit a pink-white light. Full spectrum tubes that approximate the color of natural daylight are more expensive, but the color of the light doesn't distort the color of plants and flowers.

HIGH-PRESSURE SODIUM BULB
High-pressure sodium bulbs emit light strongest at the red and orange end of the spectrum, promoting flowering. They may produce leggy growth unless used with daylight or a metal halide system. Replace them every 18 months. If your goal is to have lots of bloom, use high-pressure sodium lamps, but remember that the light has a red-orange cast and distorts the colors of everything it illuminates. It's not flattering in a living room situation.

AGROSUN GROW BULB
Agrosun gold halides are color corrected to emit more red and orange light than regular metal halides. This boosts flowering and supports compact foliar growth. Replace halide bulbs about once a year.

METAL HALIDE
Metal halide bulbs emit light strongest at the blue end of the spectrum. The result is a stark, cool-white light that produces compact, leafy growth. Because the light does not distort the colors of the plants or people it illuminates, it's a good choice for an orchid display that is part of your living area.

Growing in terrariums

Terrariums offer orchid growers an opportunity

to grow plants that need high humidity without the expense and inconvenience of a greenhouse. As Nathaniel Ward discovered in the 19th century (see Chapter 1), creating a closed environment allows you to cater to plants with special needs.

In a closed terrarium, moisture given off by orchids via transpiration stays within the airtight case. When the air inside the terrarium reaches its saturation point (relative humidity of 100 percent), water condenses out of the air and is redeposited on the plants inside the case.

This cuts down on watering, and broadens the range of orchids you can grow.

To vary the heights of your plants within the terrarium, place a few pots on top of flat rocks or on overturned pots or saucers.

Types of terrariums
Terrariums can be fashioned from any number of interesting objects: an abandoned fish tank, a large canning jar, a glass cloche, or a fancy antique Wardian case.

It might be something as simple as a single specimen plant under an antique cloche or as elaborate as a fully planted branch of epiphytic orchids inside a built-in terrarium with lights and fans.

Above: **A simple Wardian case lined with pebbles provides extra humidity for orchids.**

While a closed terrarium of any kind needs only infrequent watering (once every one to two weeks), its plants should be checked at least once a week for general health.

Enclosure terrariums

To use a glass case as an enclosure for potted plants, spread a layer of gravel 1 to 2 inches deep on the bottom of the case. This acts as a dry well and holds the roots above any extra moisture that accumulates.

Place individual pots on the gravel, being careful not to crowd them so much that it impedes air circulation.

Avoid letting foliage press against the glass. When water condenses on orchid leaves and is held there by the glass, it could burn the leaves if they are hit by strong sunlight or provide a breeding ground for fungi and bacteria.

Epiphytic terrariums

An epiphytic terrarium is a real showstopper. Choose a branch that fits inside a terrarium, then clean the branch with a 10 percent bleach, 90 percent water solution.

Add a layer of gravel to the bottom of the case and place the branch on the gravel. Branches with curves are good for this kind of display because they don't lie flat on the bottom of the gravel. This allows for better air circulation and provides different levels for planting.

Think about how your terrarium will be viewed. If the display is seen from all sides, plant the tallest specimens in the center. If the terrarium is built into a wall or up against a wall and seen only from one side, put the tallest plants at the back of the display.

It's easier to assemble an orchid branch inside the terrarium than to assemble it and then try to move it inside without damaging the orchids.

Avoid crowding the planting. Because air circulation is reduced inside closed cases, it's important to give each orchid its own space without allowing leaves to touch one another or the sides of the case.

Once they are planted and placed, water the orchids by a combination of misting and pouring a small amount of water onto the gravel at the bottom to keep humidity high.

Make a custom orchid terrarium

If you're especially handy—or know someone who is—consider building a larger setup with light tubes and fans. Because these units are self-contained, they can be placed anywhere in your home without regard to natural light.

The air inside the case dries out more quickly when you incorporate fans and lights or both, so the orchids need watering more frequently. But this is an excellent, low-maintenance way to grow high-humidity plants without a greenhouse.

Below: **Use bell jars or cloches to enclose any orchid for instant protection and extra humidity. Be careful to prevent leaves from touching the glass, which can cause them to burn in sunlight.**

gallery of orchids

Orchids that share cultural needs are called alliances. Consider them groups of relatives.

p.134
CATASETUMS
These orchids feature outstanding pendent, often fragrant, blooms.

p.136
CATTLEYAS
You may know them best as the traditional corsage orchid. Cattleyas come in many sizes, shapes, and colors.

p.149
COELOGYNES
Although coelogynes aren't as well-known as other orchid genera, many are easy to grow.

p.151
CYMBIDIUMS
If you can satisfy cymbidiums' cultural requirements, they reward you with large, long-lasting flowers.

p.156
CYPRIPEDIUMS
Water-loving slipper orchids grow luscious large, waxy flowers with distinctive pouchlike lips.

p.163
DENDROBIUMS
This genus is highly varied, containing some of the orchid world's most alluring flowers.

p.172
JEWEL ORCHIDS
Jewel orchids are prized for their extraordinary foliage and their tolerance for low light.

p.174
ONCIDIUMS
The "dancing lady" alliance contains more genera than any other, offering a wide variety of flowers.

p.187
PHALAENOPSIS
Moth orchids are the best-loved and easiest for home growers.

p.198
PLEUROTHALLIS
Pleurothallis flowers can be so tiny you need a magnifying glass to fully appreciate their exquisite detail.

p.200
VANDAS
Vandas are great for people with greenhouses or who live in tropical and subtropical climates.

p.206
SPECIAL INTEREST ORCHIDS
Some orchids are so exceptional they deserve extra mention.

Gallery of orchids

Hybridizing orchids is big business,

and the orchid family is getting larger every day. The Orchidaceae family is divided into five subfamilies, some of which are further subdivided into tribes and subtribes.

While expert growers find these terms useful, most people prefer the simpler groupings known as alliances. The alliances include naturally occurring orchids and intergeneric hybrids created by artificially crossing two or more genera. These related orchids share certain characteristics and are considered members of an alliance. Each alliance is named for its most prominent member genus: the cattleya alliance, the dendrobium alliance, the oncidium alliance, and so forth.

Once you've become familiar with an orchid genus and its typical physical traits, you can recognize it even without a plant tag. For example, if you see a sympodial orchid with large pseudobulbs producing one or two thick, stiff leaves, you know that looks like a cattleya. Wide, straplike leaves with a thick cuticle and a monopodial growth habit? Why, it must be a phalaenopsis!

Or is it? Maybe it doesn't matter. If you can narrow down an orchid's identity to its alliance, chances are you'll be able to grow it properly. It doesn't really matter if you know whether you've got a phalaenopsis or a doritaenopsis, as long as you recognize the orchid as a member of the phalaenopsis alliance. Both orchids thrive under very similar conditions, so when you understand one, you'll understand the other.

Some alliances are bigger than others. The larger groups (cattleya, dendrobium, and oncidium) exhibit more differences among members in both their physical characteristics and their cultural needs. Nonetheless, alliance members have more in common with each other than they do with orchids from other alliances.

Taxonomy changes continually

Taxonomists are biologists who classify organisms into groups. The sands of taxonomy are constantly shifting, and in the orchid world names change from year to year. Not everyone keeps up with the latest taxonomical changes, so you may see old names on plant tags. Don't worry: The names of orchids may change but the care they need doesn't.

*Above: **Phaiocalanthe Kryptonite 'Red Streak'** is a cross between a **Phaius tankervilleae** (also called nun's orchid; see page 211) and a calanthe. A terrestrial orchid, it grows and blooms with low light, and does well in moist sphagnum moss.*

Reading plant names

You may encounter a few additional bits of code when reading orchid catalogs, plant tags, or names in this gallery.

An × means a hybrid orchid. If it is an intergeneric hybrid, the × precedes the genus (× *Cattlianthe*). The × also indicates a hybrid of two species before it has been registered as a grex (*Phalaenopsis* Brother Passat × *Doritaenopsis* Brother Love Rosa).

Sib. stands for sibling. Siblings from among a grex batch are often crossed with each other to create new hybrids.

Subvar. and var. stand for subvariety and variety. These terms aren't officially part of orchid nomenclature, but you may see them used descriptively. They indicate an orchid that is a part of a group within a group. For example, var. *alba* indicates that an orchid is a white variety of an orchid that is not normally white.

Awards

You may see a group of letters following the name of an orchid. These indicate that the plant has won an award from an orchid society. Plants are judged based on standards for each genus. They compete against a standard of perfection, not against one another. The letters themselves stand for both the award that was granted and the organization granting the award.

For example, the letters FCC/AOS indicate that an orchid has received a First Class Certificate from the American Orchid Society. An FCC-winning plant has scored at least 90 points on a 100-point scale. Next is AM (Award of Merit), for orchids scoring 80–89 points, then HCC (Highly Commended Certificate), for orchids scoring 75–79 points.

Additional awards are given to exceptional plants that don't fit those criteria but show excellence in areas such as hybridization, educational value, or distinctive characteristics.

Judging orchids

AOS certified judges are volunteers who train for three to five years before achieving certification and another three to five to reach full accreditation. Judging events are scheduled monthly at numerous locations to make competition easily accessible to growers. Most orchid shows include a judging section where winning plants are exhibited.

As you might imagine, the clone of a first-class certificate winner commands a significantly higher price than an unnamed grex.

Growers take these awards seriously, as do dedicated hobbyists who want to add significant prizewinners to their collections.

TEMPERATURE REQUIREMENTS

COOL-GROWING ORCHIDS
Days 60–70°F
Nights 45–55°F

INTERMEDIATE ORCHIDS
Days 70–80°F
Nights 55–65°F

WARM-GROWING ORCHIDS
Days 80–90°F
Nights 60–70°F

Abbreviations

Abbreviations for various genera may be used in the gallery or on plant tags when you are shopping for orchids. Use this chart to decode them.

CATASETUM ALLIANCE

Catasetum	Ctsm.
Cycnoches	Cyc.
Cycnodes	Cycd.
Gongora	Gga.
Stanhopea	Stan.

CATTLEYA ALLIANCE

Brassanthe	Bsn.
Brassavola	B.
Brassocatanthe	Bct.
Brassocattleya	Bc.
Brassolaelia	Bl.
Brassolaeliocattleya	Blc.
Bratonia	Brat.
Broughtonia	Bro.
Cattleya	C.
Cattleytonia	Ctna.
Cattlianthe	Ctt.
Encyclia	E.
Epicattleya	Epc.
Epidendrum	Epi.
Guarianthe	Gur.
Guaricattonia	Gct.

Guaritonia	Grt.
Laelia	L.
Laeliocattleya	Lc.
Otaara	Otr.
Prosthechea	Psh.
Rhyncattleanthe	Rth.
Rhyncholaelia	Rl.
Rhyncholaeliocattleya	Rlc.
Rhyntonleya	Rly.
Volkertara	Vkt.

COELOGYNE ALLIANCE

Coelogyne	Coel.
Dendrochilum	Ddc.
Pleione	Pln.

CYMBIDIUM ALLIANCE

Cymbidium	Cym.

CYPRIPEDIUM ALLIANCE

Paphiopedilum	Paph.
Phragmipedium	Phrag.

DENDROBIUM ALLIANCE

Dendrobium	Den.

JEWEL ORCHID ALLIANCE

Anoectochilus	Anct.
Ludisia	Lus.
Macodes	Mac.
Stenorrhynchos	Strs.

ONCIDIUM ALLIANCE

Aliceara	Alcra.
Bakerara	Bak.
Beallara	Bllra.
Brassada	Brsa.
Brassia	Brs.
Brassidium	Brsdm.
Burrageara	Burr.
Cyrtocidium	Ctd.
Degarmoara	Dgmra.
Howeara	Hwra.
Miltassia	Mtssa.
Miltonia	Milt.
Miltonidium	Mtdm.
Miltoniopsis	Mps.
Odontioda	Oda.

Oncidium	Onc.
Oncidesa	Oncsa.
Oncidopsis	Oip.
Oncostele	Ons.
Psychopsis	Pyp.
Rhynchostele	Rst.
Rodrumnia	Rrm.
Sanderara	Sand.
Tolumnia	Tolu.
Vuylstekeara	Vuyl.
Wilsonara	Wils.

PHALAENOPSIS ALLIANCE

Doritaenopsis	Dtps.
Doritis	Dor.
Phalaenopsis	Phal.

PLEUROTHALLIS ALLIANCE

Masdevallia	Masd.
Pleurothallis	Pths.
Specklinia	Spe.

VANDA ALLIANCE

Aerangis	Aergs.
Aeridovanda	Aerdv.
Angraecum	Angcm.
Ascocenda	Ascda.
Ascocentrum	Asctm.
Euanthe	Eua.
Haraella	Hal.
Neofinetia	Neof.
Renanthera	Ren.
Rhynchostylis	Rhy.
Vanda	V.
Vascostylis	Vasco.

SPECIAL INTEREST ORCHIDS

Bifrenaria	Bif.
Bulbophylum	Bulb.
Lycaste	Lyc.
Maxillariella	Mxl.
Phaius	Phaius
Sarcochilus	Sarco.
Vanilla	Vl.
Warscewiczella	W.
Zygopetalum	Z.

Catasetum relatives

The catasetum alliance includes orchids with outstanding pendent flowers, many of them fragrant. These are high-humidity plants that grow best as mounted specimens or in orchid baskets.

Catasetum, *Cycnoches*, and the intergeneric hybrid *Cycnodes* (a cross between *Cycnoches* and *Mormodes*, another genus in the alliance) resemble one another. They are epiphytic, deciduous orchids. Thin leaves emerge from prominent nodes on thick canes shaped like spindles with papery sheaths. The nodes near the top of each cane produce clusters of multiple flowers with unusual shapes.

New growth progresses quickly—taking about six months—from emergence to flowering. Then catasetum, cycnodes, and cycnoches go dormant, losing their flowers and leaves. This can confuse beginning growers who think their orchid died when it is simply resting. During dormancy, catasetums need almost no water. During active growth, they need high humidity and should be watered frequently—as often as once a day during summer heat.

These genera have separate male and female flowers. Male catasetum flowers have a distinctive way of spreading pollen. A trigger mechanism shoots the orchid's pollinia onto the visiting bee. The pollinia stick to the bee, and the force of the shot encourages the bee to move to the next flower.

Catasetums, cycnoches, and cycnodes are warm-temperature orchids and require medium to high light. An ideal location is an unobstructed east- or west-facing window on a humidity tray. Catasetum, cycnoches, and cycnodes canes are 6 to 10 inches tall; leaves arch outward and down.

Gongora and *Stanhopea* species are epiphytic and produce pendent, usually fragrant flowers and thin, papery leaves. They are not deciduous and have recognizable pseudobulbs rather than canes shaped like spindles. Flowers grow from the base of the pseudobulbs and dangle well below the plant itself.

Stanhopea bloom spikes turn down as soon as they emerge, growing through the bark mix. They must be planted in slatted boxes with spaces large enough to allow the bloom spikes to pass through them from beneath the plant. Once the spike re-emerges into the air, the buds begin to swell.

Both *Gongora* and *Stanhopea* are intermediate-growing orchids and require medium light. They need frequent watering (every three days) during active growth.

CATASETUMS AT A GLANCE

TYPE: Sympodial, epiphyte
LIGHT: Medium to high
TEMP: Intermediate
MIX: Coarse-grain or mounted

Catasetum × roseoalbum

BLOOM: 1- to 2-inch diameter; fringed pink pouch on top of 2 white to green, sticklike sepals; 4 to 20 per spike
GROWTH HABIT: Epiphyte; sympodial; pseudobulbs shaped like spindles
LIGHT REQUIREMENT: Medium to high
TEMPERATURE REQUIREMENT: Warm
ATTRIBUTES: Unique flower shape; separate male and female flowers; pendent spikes emerge from base of pseudobulbs

Cycnoches chlorochilon

BLOOM: 2- to 6-inch diameter; fleshy; yellow to green; white lip with dark green accent at base; 1 to 6 flowers per arching spike; 1 to 2 spikes per pseudobulb
GROWTH HABIT: Epiphyte; sympodial; pseudobulbs shaped like spindles
LIGHT REQUIREMENT: Medium to high
TEMPERATURE REQUIREMENT: Warm
ATTRIBUTES: Separate male and female flowers; requires dry winter rest

Cycnodes Wine Delight

BLOOM: 3- to 6-inch diameter; deep ruby red; many flowers per arching spike; 1 to 2 spikes per pseudobulb

GROWTH HABIT: Epiphyte; sympodial; pseudobulbs shaped like spindles

LIGHT REQUIREMENT: Medium to high

TEMPERATURE REQUIREMENT: Intermediate to warm

ATTRIBUTES: Separate male and female flowers; requires dry winter rest

Gongora quinquenervis

BLOOM: 3-inch diameter; yellow speckled with reddish-brown; yellow lip; multiflowered, pendent bloom spike to 30 inches

GROWTH HABIT: Epiphyte; sympodial; pseudobulbs

LIGHT REQUIREMENT: Medium

TEMPERATURE REQUIREMENT: Intermediate

ATTRIBUTES: Fragrant; easy bloom

Gongora rufescens

BLOOM: Yellow with red speckles; 2-inch diameter; multiflowered, pendent bloom spike can reach up to 30 inches

GROWTH HABIT: Epiphyte; sympodial; pseudobulbs

LIGHT REQUIREMENT: Medium

TEMPERATURE REQUIREMENT: Intermediate to warm

ATTRIBUTES: Fragrant

Stanhopea hernandezii

BLOOM: 2- to 4-inch diameter; pale yellow, spotted with maroon; white lip also spotted with maroon; 2 to 4 blooms per spike

GROWTH HABIT: Epiphyte; sympodial; pseudobulbs

LIGHT REQUIREMENT: Medium to high

TEMPERATURE REQUIREMENT: Cool to intermediate

ATTRIBUTES: Strong scent; pendent bloom spikes; multiple spikes per plant

Cattleya relatives
While the various genera that compose this alliance can be different in size, flower color, and scent, they have much in common. When described as a group, they are sometimes referred to collectively as cattleyas. Smaller plants are called minicatts.

CATTLEYAS AT A GLANCE

TYPE: Sympodial, epiphyte
LIGHT: Medium to high
TEMP: Intermediate
MIX: Medium- to coarse-grain or mounted

The cattleya alliance includes many genera including: *Cattleya, Brassavola, Broughtonia, Encyclia, Epidendrum, Guarianthe, Laelia,* and *Rhyncholaelia*. Members of the alliance cross easily with one another, and there are many intergeneric hybrids, with the most common listed on this page.

The recent elimination of the genus *Sophronitis* resulted in the renaming of many related orchids and the abolition of several manmade genera that included *Sophronitis* as a parent. While you may still see *Potinara, Rolfeara,* and *Hawkinsara* on plant tags, those names are no longer officially in use.

Members of the genus *Cattleya* are used as traditional corsage orchids. The blooms are large, lasting for about two or three weeks, and many are fragrant. Flower colors are rich and saturated, and the petals may be striped, speckled, or solid. The orchid lip usually contrasts with the rest of the flower.

Cattleyas are sympodial epiphytes and are generally quite drought-tolerant. One or two thick leaves emerge from pseudobulbs. They have thick velamen roots and grow best potted in medium- to coarse-grain bark mix or as mounted specimens.

Allow them to dry out between waterings. Begin by watering once a week, then adjust according to your specific growing conditions.

Cattleyas are medium- to high-light orchids. They require bright sun if grown behind glass, although if placed against a south-facing window they may get sunburned. In this situation, pull plants back a foot from the window or hang a sheer curtain during the middle of the day. Outdoors, they should be given protection from the sun's strongest rays.

Foliage should be medium to light green. Dark green leaves indicate a light deficiency and yellowish leaves show that the plant is getting too much sun.

Cattleyas are generally midsize plants, with foliage from 12 to 24 inches tall. Minicatts range from 6 to 12 inches. They are intermediate-temperature orchids.

Intergeneric hybrids
These are the most common cattleya intergeneric hybrids a home grower is likely to encounter on orchid labels and in catalogs.

BRASSANTHE: *Brassavola × Guarianthe*
BRASSOCATANTHE:
Brassavola × Cattleya × Guarianthe
BRASSOCATTLEYA: *Brassavola × Cattleya*
BRASSOLAELIA: *Brassavola × Laelia*
BRASSOLAELIOCATTLEYA:
Brassavola × Cattleya × Laelia
CATTLEYTONIA: *Broughtonia × Cattleya*
CATTLIANTHE: *Cattleya × Guarianthe*
EPICATTLEYA: *Cattleya × Epidendrum*
GUARICATTONIA:
Broughtonia × Cattleya × Guarianthe
GUARITONIA: *Broughtonia × Guarianthe*
LAELIOCATONIA: *Broughtonia × Cattleya × Laelia*
LAELIOCATTLEYA: *Cattleya × Laelia*
OTAARA:
Brassavola × Broughtonia × Cattleya × Laelia
RHYNCATTLEANTHE:
Cattleya × Guarinathe × Rhyncholaelia
RHYNCHOLAELIOCATTLEYA:
Cattleya × Rhyncolaelia
RHYNTONLEYA: *Cattleytonia × Rhyncholaelia*
VOLKERTARA:
Broughtonia × Cattleya × Guarianthe × Rhyncholaelia

Rhyncattleanthe Momilani Rainbow is an example of an intergeneric hybrid in the cattleya alliance.

Brassanthe Maikai 'Lea' × *Cattleya* Triumph #2

BLOOM: 3- to 5-inch diameter; light pink to purple; darker lip flushed with white; 1 to 4 per spike

GROWTH HABIT: Epiphyte; sympodial; cylindrical pseudobulbs

LIGHT REQUIREMENT: High

TEMPERATURE REQUIREMENT: Intermediate to warm

ATTRIBUTES: Fragrant; multiple spikes; long-lasting bloom

Brassavola nodosa

BLOOM: 3- to 4-inch diameter; white and green; 1 to 5 flowers per spike

GROWTH HABIT: Epiphyte; sympodial; narrow, cylindrical pseudobulbs

LIGHT REQUIREMENT: High

TEMPERATURE REQUIREMENT: Warm

ATTRIBUTES: Strong, sweet fragrance; drought tolerant; low maintenance; easy bloom

Brassocatanthe Lemon Yellow 'Carib'

BLOOM: 3- to 4-inch diameter; yellow; orange speckled lip; 3 to 8 flowers per spike

GROWTH HABIT: Epiphyte; sympodial; pseudobulbs

LIGHT REQUIREMENT: High

TEMPERATURE REQUIREMENT: Intermediate

ATTRIBUTES: Vivid saturated flower color; drought tolerant; multiple spikes

Brassocattleya Morning Glory

BLOOM: 3- to 4-inch diameter; white to pink; dark pink to purple striped lip; 2 to 5 flowers per spike

GROWTH HABIT: Epiphyte; sympodial; narrow, cylindrical pseudobulbs

LIGHT REQUIREMENT: High

TEMPERATURE REQUIREMENT: Intermediate to warm

ATTRIBUTES: Sweet, candy scent; drought tolerant

Cattleya aclandiae 'Iguassu' × 'Valley Isle'

BLOOM: 3- to 4-inch diameter; yellow to green petals with maroon spots; pink lip; 1 to 3 per spike

GROWTH HABIT: Epiphyte; sympodial; cylindrical pseudobulbs

LIGHT REQUIREMENT: High

TEMPERATURE REQUIREMENT: Warm

ATTRIBUTES: Fragrant; drought tolerant

Cattleya amethystoglossa

BLOOM: 2- to 4-inch diameter, white to pink with purple spots; magenta ruffled lip; 2 to 10 per spike

GROWTH HABIT: Epiphyte or lithophyte; sympodial; cylindrical pseudobulbs

LIGHT REQUIREMENT: Medium to high

TEMPERATURE REQUIREMENT: Intermediate to warm

ATTRIBUTES: Drought tolerant; lightly fragrant

Cattleya Janet × Rhyncholaeliocattleya Magnificent Obsession

BLOOM: 3- to 6-inch diameter; magenta; dark splashes on outer petals; dark lip with white center; 1 to 3 flowers per spike

GROWTH HABIT: Epiphyte; sympodial

LIGHT REQUIREMENT: Medium to high

TEMPERATURE REQUIREMENT: Cool to intermediate

ATTRIBUTES: Vibrant color; multiple spikes

Cattleya lueddemanniana

BLOOM: 5- to 8-inch diameter; lavender to purple; darker, ruffled, tubular lip; 1 to 3 per spike

GROWTH HABIT: Epiphyte; sympodial; pseudobulbs

LIGHT REQUIREMENT: Medium to high

TEMPERATURE REQUIREMENT: Warm

ATTRIBUTES: Fragrant; drought tolerant

Cattleya mossiae

BLOOM: 5- to 8-inch diameter; white, pink, or lilac; darker, ruffled lip with yellow or orange center; 2 to 4 per spike
GROWTH HABIT: Epiphyte; sympodial; pseudobulbs
LIGHT REQUIREMENT: Medium to high
TEMPERATURE REQUIREMENT: Intermediate
ATTRIBUTES: Lightly fragrant; drought tolerant

Cattleya percivaliana

BLOOM: 5-inch diameter; pink to lilac; dramatically darker, ruffled lip; 2 to 4 per spike
GROWTH HABIT: Lithophyte or epiphyte; sympodial; pseudobulbs
LIGHT REQUIREMENT: High
TEMPERATURE REQUIREMENT: Intermediate
ATTRIBUTES: Fragrant; drought tolerant

Cattleya Summer Spot 'Carmela'

BLOOM: 3- to 5-inch diameter; pink with purple spots; white-and-pink flared lip; 2 per spike
GROWTH HABIT: Epiphyte; sympodial; pseudobulbs
LIGHT REQUIREMENT: High
TEMPERATURE REQUIREMENT: Intermediate
ATTRIBUTES: Lightly fragrant; drought tolerant

Cattleya Tangerine Jewel × Cosmic Delite

BLOOM: 2-inch diameter, orange to vermilion; darker lip striped with yellow; 1 to 3 per spike; cultivars highly variable
GROWTH HABIT: Epiphyte; sympodial; pseudobulbs
LIGHT REQUIREMENT: Medium
TEMPERATURE REQUIREMENT: Cool to intermediate
ATTRIBUTES: Excellent color

Cattleya violacea

BLOOM: 3- to 4-inch diameter; purple to pink; deep-purple-and-yellow lip; 3 to 5 per spike

GROWTH HABIT: Epiphyte; sympodial; pseudobulbs shaped like spindles

LIGHT REQUIREMENT: Medium to high

TEMPERATURE REQUIREMENT: Warm

ATTRIBUTES: Fragrant; drought tolerant; long-lasting bloom

Cattleya walkeriana

BLOOM: 3- to 5-inch diameter; pink to purple; darker lip streaked with yellow; 1 to 2 per spike

GROWTH HABIT: Epiphyte; sympodial; cylindrical pseudobulbs

LIGHT REQUIREMENT: Medium to high

TEMPERATURE REQUIREMENT: Intermediate

ATTRIBUTES: Fragrant; drought tolerant; long-lasting bloom

Cattleytonia Koolau Sunset 'Hawaii'

BLOOM: 2- to 4-inch diameter; deep red; white center; 1 to 4 per spike

GROWTH HABIT: Epiphyte; sympodial; pseudobulbs

LIGHT REQUIREMENT: High

TEMPERATURE REQUIREMENT: Cool to intermediate

ATTRIBUTES: Velvety flowers; saturated color

Cattlianthe Gold Digger 'Orchid Jungle'

BLOOM: 3-inch diameter; yellow with vermilion lip; 3 to 6 blooms per spike

GROWTH HABIT: Epiphyte; sympodial; pseudobulbs

LIGHT REQUIREMENT: High

TEMPERATURE REQUIREMENT: Cool to intermediate

ATTRIBUTES: Long-lasting bloom

Cattlianthe Hawaiian Blue Sky 'Chelsea' × *Cattleya* Mini Purple var. *coerulea*

BLOOM: 4- to 5-inch diameter; lavender; purple lip; 2 to 4 per spike

GROWTH HABIT: Epiphyte; sympodial; cylindrical pseudobulbs

LIGHT REQUIREMENT: High

TEMPERATURE REQUIREMENT: Cool to warm

ATTRIBUTES: Fragrant; multiple spikes; long lasting

Cattlianthe Hazel Boyd 'Elizabeth' subvar. 'Debbie'

BLOOM: 3- to 4-inch diameter; saturated orange-red; 2 to 3 per spike

GROWTH HABIT: Epiphyte; sympodial; pseudobulbs

LIGHT REQUIREMENT: Medium to high

TEMPERATURE REQUIREMENT: Cool to intermediate

ATTRIBUTES: Vibrant color; may be sold as *Cattlianthe* Hazel Boyd 'Debbie'

Cattlianthe Jean's Winter Gold

BLOOM: 2- to 3-inch diameter; lavender sepals; purple-and-lavender petals; ruffled lip with white and yellow center; 4 to 6 per spike

GROWTH HABIT: Epiphyte; sympodial; cylindrical pseudobulbs

LIGHT REQUIREMENT: High

TEMPERATURE REQUIREMENT: Cool to intermediate

ATTRIBUTES: Excellent color combination; multiple spikes

Cattlianthe Rojo

BLOOM: 2- to 2½-inch diameter; vermilion; lip flushed with yellow and speckled with vermilion; 4 to 12 per spike

GROWTH HABIT: Epiphyte; sympodial; pseudobulbs

LIGHT REQUIREMENT: High

TEMPERATURE REQUIREMENT: Cool to intermediate

ATTRIBUTES: Multiple spikes

Cattlianthe Tutankhamen 'Pop'

BLOOM: 3- to 4-inch diameter; deep ruby red; lip flushed with yellow; 3 to 7 per spike

GROWTH HABIT: Epiphyte; sympodial; pseudobulbs

LIGHT REQUIREMENT: High

TEMPERATURE REQUIREMENT: Cool to intermediate

ATTRIBUTES: Fragrant; rich color

Cattlianthe Warpaint 'Sun Bulb'

BLOOM: 3- to 3½-inch diameter; deep rosy red; lip flushed with yellow; 2 to 5 per spike

GROWTH HABIT: Epiphyte; sympodial; pseudobulbs

LIGHT REQUIREMENT: High

TEMPERATURE REQUIREMENT: Cool to intermediate

ATTRIBUTES: Wavy petal margins; multiple spikes

Encyclia alata

BLOOM: 2-inch diameter; yellow to green and purple; white lip striped with purple and edged with yellow; branching spikes with as many as 20 flowers

GROWTH HABIT: Epiphyte; sympodial; pseudobulbs

LIGHT REQUIREMENT: Medium to high

TEMPERATURE REQUIREMENT: Intermediate

ATTRIBUTES: Fragrant; long-lasting blooms

Encyclia expansa

BLOOM: 2-inch diameter; pale green and brown; flared magenta lip; 5 to 20 on branching spike

GROWTH HABIT: Epiphyte; sympodial; pseudobulbs

LIGHT REQUIREMENT: Medium to high

TEMPERATURE REQUIREMENT: Intermediate to warm

ATTRIBUTES: Graceful, arching bloom spike

Epicattleya
René Marqués 'Tyler'

BLOOM: 2- to 3½-inch diameter; green; flared yellow
  lip with magenta center; 3 to 6 per spike
GROWTH HABIT: Epiphyte; sympodial; cylindrical
  pseudobulbs
LIGHT REQUIREMENT: Medium to high
TEMPERATURE REQUIREMENT: Cool to warm
ATTRIBUTES: Remarkable color combination;
  multiple spikes

Epidendrum Ballerina

BLOOM: 1-inch diameter; yellow, orange, red, pink;
  fringed lip; dense clusters of as many as
  25 flowers per spike
GROWTH HABIT: Epiphyte; sympodial; cylindrical
  pseudobulbs
LIGHT REQUIREMENT: High
TEMPERATURE REQUIREMENT: Intermediate
  to warm
ATTRIBUTES: Multiple tall spikes per plant; also sold
  as *Epidendrum radicans* 'Ballerina'

Epidendrum ciliare

BLOOM: 3-inch diameter; pale green linear petals;
  white fringed lip; 2 to 8 per spike
GROWTH HABIT: Epiphyte; sympodial;
  cylindrical pseudobulbs
LIGHT REQUIREMENT: Medium to high
TEMPERATURE REQUIREMENT: Intermediate
ATTRIBUTES: Fragrant; unusual flower shape

Epidendrum coriifolium
'Sycamore Creek'

BLOOM: 1½-inch diameter; green faintly flushed with
  purple; 2 to 16 per spike
GROWTH HABIT: Epiphyte; sympodial; cylindrical
  pseudobulbs
LIGHT REQUIREMENT: Medium
TEMPERATURE REQUIREMENT: Cool to
  intermediate
ATTRIBUTES: Unusual flower color; bushy flower spike;
  multiple spikes per plant

Epidendrum Hokulea

BLOOM: 1- to 2-inch diameter; vermilion; fringed and lobed yellow lip; dense clusters of as many as 30 flowers per spike

GROWTH HABIT: Epiphyte; sympodial; cylindrical pseudobulbs

LIGHT REQUIREMENT: High

TEMPERATURE REQUIREMENT: Intermediate to warm

ATTRIBUTES: Multiple spikes per plant

Epidendrum stamfordianum

BLOOM: 2-inch diameter; yellow with red spots; flared, lobed white lip; bloom spike branching, many-flowered

GROWTH HABIT: Epiphyte; sympodial; cylindrical pseudobulbs

LIGHT REQUIREMENT: Medium to high

TEMPERATURE REQUIREMENT: Intermediate

ATTRIBUTES: Fragrant; long-lasting bloom; multiple pendent spikes per plant

Guarianthe aurantiaca

BLOOM: 1- to 2-inch diameter; orange to red petals with a few red speckles; 3 to 7 per spike

GROWTH HABIT: Epiphyte; sympodial; pseudobulbs

LIGHT REQUIREMENT: Medium to high

TEMPERATURE REQUIREMENT: Intermediate to warm

ATTRIBUTES: Intensely bright flower color; drought tolerant; easy to grow and bloom; formerly known as *Cattleya aurantiaca*

Guarianthe Hail Storm 'Coconut Orchids'

BLOOM: 3- to 4-inch diameter; magenta flushed with pink; dark tubular lip accented with white; 2 to 12 per spike

GROWTH HABIT: Epiphyte; sympodial; pseudobulbs

LIGHT REQUIREMENT: High

TEMPERATURE REQUIREMENT: Intermediate to warm

ATTRIBUTES: Multiple spikes per plant

Guaritonia 'Why Not'

BLOOM: 2-inch diameter; deep red with yellow center; 3 to 7 per spike

GROWTH HABIT: Epiphyte; sympodial; pseudobulbs

LIGHT REQUIREMENT: High

TEMPERATURE REQUIREMENT: Intermediate

ATTRIBUTES: Easy bloomer; multiple spikes per plant

Laelia anceps 'SanBar Super Splash'

BLOOM: Lavender sepals; purple to magenta petals splashed with lavender; ruffled lip flushed with yellow; 2 to 5 per spike

GROWTH HABIT: Epiphyte or lithophyte; sympodial; pseudobulbs

LIGHT REQUIREMENT: High

TEMPERATURE REQUIREMENT: Intermediate

ATTRIBUTES: Extraordinary color and pattern

Laeliocattleya Rock Ruby

BLOOM: 2- to 3-inch diameter; rich purple to pink; ruffled tubular lip with yellow interior; 2 to 5 per spike

GROWTH HABIT: Epiphyte; sympodial; pseudobulbs

LIGHT REQUIREMENT: Intermediate to high

TEMPERATURE REQUIREMENT: Medium

ATTRIBUTES: Multiple spikes per plant

Prosthechea cochleata

BLOOM: 2- to 3-inch diameter; cream and purple; cockleshell lip on top of tentacles; 2 to 20 blooms per spike

GROWTH HABIT: Epiphyte; sympodial; pseudobulbs

LIGHT REQUIREMENT: Medium

TEMPERATURE REQUIREMENT: Intermediate to warm

ATTRIBUTES: Unusual bloom shape; repeat bloom; easy to grow

Prosthechea cochleata × Prosthechea vitellina

BLOOM: 1- to 2-inch diameter; yellow; cockleshell lip striped with purple; 2 to 9 per spike

GROWTH HABIT: Epiphyte; sympodial; pseudobulbs

LIGHT REQUIREMENT: Medium

TEMPERATURE REQUIREMENT: Intermediate

ATTRIBUTES: Unusual flower; long-lasting bloom; multiple spikes per plant; highly variable within grex

Rhyncattleanthe Fuchs Orange Nuggett

BLOOM: 3-inch diameter; yellow to orange; 2 to 4 per spike

GROWTH HABIT: Epiphyte; sympodial; pseudobulbs

LIGHT REQUIREMENT: High

TEMPERATURE REQUIREMENT: Cool to intermediate

ATTRIBUTES: Drought tolerant; multiple spikes per plant

Rhyncattleanthe Lily Marie Almas

BLOOM: 3- to 4-inch diameter; deep orange; ruffled yellow lip; 3 to 5 per spike

GROWTH HABIT: Epiphyte; sympodial; pseudobulbs

LIGHT REQUIREMENT: High

TEMPERATURE REQUIREMENT: Cool to intermediate

ATTRIBUTES: Multiple spikes per plant; repeat bloom

Rhyncholaeliocattleya Dick Smith 'Paradise'

BLOOM: 3-inch diameter; peach sepals; ruffled yellow petals splashed with magenta; 2 to 3 per spike

GROWTH HABIT: Epiphyte; sympodial; pseudobulbs

LIGHT REQUIREMENT: High

TEMPERATURE REQUIREMENT: Cool to intermediate

ATTRIBUTES: Colorful bloom; multiple spikes per plant; formerly *Potinara*

Rhyncholaeliocattleya
Haadyai Delight 'Bang Prom Gold' × *Rlc.* Krull's Lemonade

BLOOM: 6-inch diameter; yellow; large ruffled lip striped with orange; 1 to 3 per spike

GROWTH HABIT: Epiphyte; sympodial; pseudobulbs

LIGHT REQUIREMENT: High

TEMPERATURE REQUIREMENT: Cool to intermediate

ATTRIBUTES: Large flowers; long-lasting bloom

Rhyncholaeliocattleya
Haw Yuan Gold

BLOOM: 6- to 8-inch diameter; rich yellow; large ruffled lip flushed with orange; 1 to 2 per spike

GROWTH HABIT: Epiphyte; sympodial; pseudobulbs

LIGHT REQUIREMENT: High

TEMPERATURE REQUIREMENT: Cool to intermediate

ATTRIBUTES: Large, vibrant flowers; formerly *Potinara*

Rhyncholaeliocattleya
Lawless Zauberflote 'Apricot'

BLOOM: 4- to 6-inch diameter; peach petals; large ruffled magenta-and-yellow lip; 1 to 3 per spike

GROWTH HABIT: Epiphyte; sympodial; pseudobulbs

LIGHT REQUIREMENT: High

TEMPERATURE REQUIREMENT: Cool to intermediate

ATTRIBUTES: Large, vibrant flowers

Rhyncholaeliocattleya
Mahina Yahiro 'Ulii'

BLOOM: 4- to 6-inch diameter; pink to purple; large, ruffled lip with yellow center; 1 to 3 per spike

GROWTH HABIT: Epiphyte; sympodial; pseudobulbs

LIGHT REQUIREMENT: High

TEMPERATURE REQUIREMENT: Cool to intermediate

ATTRIBUTES: Large flowers; multiple spikes per plant; long-lasting bloom

Coelogyne relatives

The coelogyne alliance includes the genera *Coelogyne*, *Dendrochilum*, and *Pleione*, among others. All are epiphytes with thin leaves.

Coelogyne orchids are sympodial epiphytes. They require medium light and may be cool, intermediate, or warm growing, depending on the species or cultivar. All grow best with a rest period after flowering. Plants may have one or multiple flowers; many are quite fragrant. Those with pendent flowers should be hung to best show off their bloom. Coelogynes thrive in coarse-grain bark mix and as bark-mounted specimens, but since they don't like transplanting, bark mounting may be the best choice. They may reach 6 to 24 inches in height.

Dendrochilum orchids are sympodial epiphytes with pseudobulbs that each produce a single leaf. They have long inflorescences composed of many tiny flowers that are often fragrant. These evergreen orchids grow best in fine- to medium-grain bark and medium light. They are cool, intermediate, and warm growing, depending on the species. Dendrochilums range from 4 to 24 inches tall.

Most pleiones are cool growing. They are deciduous, terrestrial, sympodial miniatures and require medium to high light. Pleiones are miniature orchids, reaching a maximum of about 12 inches tall. They should be grown in fine-grain bark mix. They thrive when potbound and used to be potted in low pots due to their shallow root systems. However, new research shows they adapt nicely to normal-size containers. Their flower size is large in proportion to plant size. The lips of many pleiones are fringed. Inflorescences emerge from the top of pseudobulbs and bear one or two flowers. They have an unusual appearance: large flowers perched on top of small, leafless pseudobulbs. Leaves drop a few months after flowering is done, signaling the beginning of dormancy. Withhold water and food until new growth appears or spring begins, whichever comes first. New pseudobulbs appear in spring and should flower the second year.

COELOGYNES AT A GLANCE

TYPE: Sympodial, epiphyte
LIGHT: Medium to high
TEMP: Cool, intermediate, or warm
MIX: Fine- to coarse-grain or mounted

Coelogyne flaccida

BLOOM: 1- to 2-inch diameter; white; lip marked with yellow and red; 3 to 10 blooms per spike
GROWTH HABIT: Epiphyte or lithophyte; sympodial; pseudobulbs
LIGHT REQUIREMENT: Medium
TEMPERATURE REQUIREMENT: Cool to intermediate
ATTRIBUTES: Unusual fragrance; pendent bloom

Coelogyne Memoria Louis Forget 'Mystery'

BLOOM: 3- to 4-inch diameter; white to pink; large lip mostly orange-red; 3 to 5 blooms per spike; dorsal sepal curves into center of bloom
GROWTH HABIT: Epiphyte or lithophyte; sympodial; pseudobulbs
LIGHT REQUIREMENT: Medium
TEMPERATURE REQUIREMENT: Cool to intermediate
ATTRIBUTES: Striking color contrast; interesting shape

Coelogyne Memoria Sadako

BLOOM: 3- to 4-inch diameter; white subtly streaked with yellow; large orange to red lip tipped with yellow; 3 to 5 blooms per spike

GROWTH HABIT: Epiphyte; sympodial; pseudobulbs

LIGHT REQUIREMENT: Medium

TEMPERATURE REQUIREMENT: Cool to intermediate

ATTRIBUTES: Compact plant; striking color contrast

Dendrochilum magnum

BLOOM: ¼- to ½-inch diameter; white and yellow; numerous flowers on arching bloom spikes

GROWTH HABIT: Epiphyte; sympodial; pseudobulbs

LIGHT REQUIREMENT: Medium

TEMPERATURE REQUIREMENT: Intermediate

ATTRIBUTES: Fragrant; multiple long bloom spikes per plant

Dendrochilum wenzelii

BLOOM: ¼- to ½-inch diameter; red; numerous flowers on bloom spike

GROWTH HABIT: Epiphyte; sympodial; pseudobulbs

LIGHT REQUIREMENT: Medium

TEMPERATURE REQUIREMENT: Intermediate to warm

ATTRIBUTES: Multiple spikes per plant

Pleione formosana

BLOOM: 3- to 4-inch diameter; lavender; pale, fringed tubular lip with yellow to brown markings; flowers borne single, rarely 2 per spike

GROWTH HABIT: Lithophyte, epiphyte, or terrestrial; sympodial; pseudobulbs; deciduous

LIGHT REQUIREMENT: Medium to high

TEMPERATURE REQUIREMENT: Cool

ATTRIBUTES: Large flower on compact plant; slightly fragrant; multiple spikes per plant

Cymbidium relatives

While there are other genera in the cymbidium alliance, cymbidiums are the most popular for home growers. Cymbidiums have a reputation for being difficult to bloom indoors in certain parts of the country, but if you can satisfy their cultural requirements, they reward you with large, long-lasting flowers in green, yellow, orange, pink, white, or red. Blooms may be spotted, striped, or picotee, and the lips are usually contrasting.

There are three cymbidium groups differentiated by their flower size and optimum growing temperatures. The terminology can be confusing because some growers describe their orchids differently.

Group 1 cymbidiums are large-flowered types sometimes called standard cymbidiums. They are 2- to 3-foot-tall, beefy plants. They are cool-growing orchids, tolerating nighttime temperatures as low as 40°F. Daytime temperatures higher than 80°F inhibit blooms. You may see them growing outdoors in places like coastal California where temperatures stay above freezing in winter and below 90°F in summer. They generally bloom in winter and spring. Their inflorescences can be upright or arching.

Group 2 cymbidiums are small-flowered tropical and subtropical orchids that tolerate somewhat higher temperatures, up to 86°F during the day, and 65 to 68°F at night. They bloom in summer.

Group 3 cymbidiums are small-flowered temperate orchids. They are cool growing and bloom in winter and early spring.

The small-flowered types (Groups 2 and 3) are sometimes grouped as miniatures. They may have upright, arching, or pendent flowers.

You may also hear the term "oriental cymbidiums." These are orchids that originate in Asia. They may be fragrant and have variegated foliage. Although they are sometimes lumped in with miniatures, neither the term miniature nor oriental tells you much about cultural requirements. To know the category of your small-flowered cymbidium, ask the grower or research the orchid online or in a book.

Recent hybridization has produced teacup hybrids that are true miniatures in flower size and in overall plant size—less than 12 inches tall.

Cascading hybrids are also popular, with heavy flower pendants best exhibited in a hanging basket. Cascading hybrids are by definition miniatures, but a miniature cymbidium can still be a substantial plant.

All cymbidiums are high-light orchids. With inadequate light they grow but don't bloom. For large-flowered (standard) types, cool night temperatures in autumn are also crucial for blooming. Many growers leave their cymbidiums outdoors from late summer until a few weeks before the first frost to give the plants the temperature fluctuation they need.

In nature cymbidiums are either epiphytic or terrestrial. They have thick pseudobulbs. In pots, cymbidiums grow best in a fine-grain bark mix. They produce long-lasting flowers on long spikes, 15 to 30 blooms per stem.

Cymbidiums grow anywhere from 6 inches (teacup size) to 36 inches tall (standards), not counting flower spikes.

CYMBIDIUMS AT A GLANCE

TYPE: Sympodial, terrestrial
LIGHT: High
TEMP: Cool to intermediate
MIX: Fine-grain bark

Cymbidium Chen's Ruby

BLOOM: 4-inch diameter; orange striped with red; ruffled lip with red dots; 5 to 20 per spike
GROWTH HABIT: Terrestrial; sympodial; Group 2
LIGHT REQUIREMENT: Medium to high
TEMPERATURE REQUIREMENT: Intermediate
ATTRIBUTES: Fragrant; intricate pattern

This large-flowered rosy-pink cymbidium NOID is an example of a Group 1 cymbidium.

Cymbidium Crescent Tears (Lady Mini × Lucky Flower)

BLOOM: 3-inch diameter; bright yellow; red pattern on lower lip; 10 to 40 per spike

GROWTH HABIT: Terrestrial; sympodial; Group 1

LIGHT REQUIREMENT: High

TEMPERATURE REQUIREMENT: Cool to intermediate

ATTRIBUTES: Very floriferous; tightly clustered blooms; some consider this a Group 3 miniature

Cymbidium Flirtation

BLOOM: 3-inch diameter; yellow; pale yellow ruffled lip; 10 to 20 per spike

GROWTH HABIT: Terrestrial; sympodial; Group 3

LIGHT REQUIREMENT: High

TEMPERATURE REQUIREMENT: Cool to intermediate

ATTRIBUTES: Miniature; multiple spikes per plant

Cymbidium King Arthur

BLOOM: 3- to 3½-inch diameter; yellow; white ruffled lip marked with red; 5 to 15 per spike

GROWTH HABIT: Terrestrial; sympodial; Group 2

LIGHT REQUIREMENT: High

TEMPERATURE REQUIREMENT: Intermediate

ATTRIBUTES: Miniature; strong color variation within grex

Cymbidium Lady Fire 'Red Angelica'

BLOOM: 4-inch diameter, deep rosy red with darker veins; white ruffled lip with red markings; 5 to 15 per spike

GROWTH HABIT: Terrestrial; sympodial; Group 1

LIGHT REQUIREMENT: High

TEMPERATURE REQUIREMENT: Cool to intermediate

ATTRIBUTES: Rich colors; subtle pattern

Cymbidium lowianum 'James Drysdale'

BLOOM: 3- to 4½-inch diameter; yellow; white lip marked with red; 15 to 30 per spike

GROWTH HABIT: Epiphyte; sympodial; pseudobulbs; Group 1

LIGHT REQUIREMENT: High

TEMPERATURE REQUIREMENT: Cool

ATTRIBUTES: Unusual shape; sometimes slightly fragrant

Cymbidium Memoria Connie Jo Nine

BLOOM: 2-inch diameter; bright red with thin white margins; orange ruffled lip with maroon blotches; arching to pendent bloom; 15 to 35 per spike

GROWTH HABIT: Terrestrial; sympodial; Group 2

LIGHT REQUIREMENT: High

TEMPERATURE REQUIREMENT: Cool to warm

ATTRIBUTES: Highly floriferous; vibrant flower color

Cymbidium Mount Vision 'Hallelujah'

BLOOM: 4- to 5-inch diameter; pale pink with dark pink splotches; ruffled lip with dark pink markings, flushed with yellow; 5 to 10 per spike

GROWTH HABIT: Terrestrial; sympodial; Group 1

LIGHT REQUIREMENT: High

TEMPERATURE REQUIREMENT: Cool to intermediate

ATTRIBUTES: Large flower; intricate pattern; delicate colors

Cymbidium Piñata 'SanBar Black Hole'

BLOOM: 5-inch diameter; orange with red spots and veins; red ruffled lip; 5 to 10 per spike

GROWTH HABIT: Terrestrial; sympodial; Group 1

LIGHT REQUIREMENT: High

TEMPERATURE REQUIREMENT: Cool to intermediate

ATTRIBUTES: Showy colors and pattern; large flower

Cymbidium Rhythm

BLOOM: 4-inch diameter; chartreuse; white ruffled
lip with red markings flushed with yellow;
10 to 20 per spike
GROWTH HABIT: Terrestrial; sympodial; Group 1
LIGHT REQUIREMENT: High
TEMPERATURE REQUIREMENT: Cool
to intermediate
ATTRIBUTES: Many-flowered; unusual colors;
high color contrast

Cymbidium sanderae

BLOOM: 3-inch diameter; white; ruffled lip
with maroon markings flushed with yellow;
10 to 15 per spike
GROWTH HABIT: Terrestrial; sympodial; Group 1
LIGHT REQUIREMENT: High
TEMPERATURE REQUIREMENT: Intermediate
ATTRIBUTES: Fragrant; outstanding color contrast

Cymbidium Tapestry 'Fire Dawn'

BLOOM: 4- to 5-inch diameter; orange with darker
orange veins flushed with yellow; white ruffled lip
with red markings; 5 to 15 per spike
GROWTH HABIT: Terrestrial; sympodial; Group 1
LIGHT REQUIREMENT: High
TEMPERATURE REQUIREMENT: Cool
to intermediate
ATTRIBUTES: Vibrant colors; large bloom

Cymbidium tortisepalum var. longibracteatum 'Faye Wong'

BLOOM: 2- to 3-inch diameter; pale green petals;
sepals with red stripes; white lip with red markings;
1 to 3 per short spike
GROWTH HABIT: Terrestrial; sympodial; Group 2
LIGHT REQUIREMENT: High
TEMPERATURE REQUIREMENT: Intermediate
ATTRIBUTES: Miniature; fragrant; also sold as
C. goeringii var. longibracteatum

Cypripedium relatives

Cypripediums are the slipper orchids. The most popular genera for home orchid growers are *Paphiopedilum* and *Phragmipedium*. Both have luscious, large, waxy flowers with distinctive pouchlike lips. Neither genus forms pseudobulbs. The foliage is held in tight fans.

CYPRIPEDIUMS AT A GLANCE

TYPE: Sympodial, terrestrial
LIGHT: Low to medium
TEMP: Cool to intermediate to warm
MIX: Fine-grain bark

Paphiopedilums (also called paphs) have not yet been successfully propagated by cloning. All plants are either collected from the wild or grown from seed. They are divided into two groups: those with solid green leaves and those with mottled leaves. Generally, green-leaved paphiopedilums are cool growing and mottled-leaved paphs are warm growing. Both are fairly adaptable to other conditions. These orchids need water two or three times a week in summer and once a week in winter. They like high humidity and grow best in a fine-grain bark mix.

In nature, paphiopedilums are shade lovers. They are terrestrials, with some of the lowest light needs for home growing. They tolerate morning sun but should be protected from sun in the middle of the day.

Too much light results in yellow foliage and may burn leaves, leaving brown spots. Put a paphiopedilum in an east window. If you must keep it in a south- or west-facing window, protect it with a sheer curtain. Plants may bloom in bright, unobstructed north windows.

Flowers are produced on stems 8 to 18 inches long, usually singly and sometimes in pairs. They can last for two months and come in many colors, including yellow, rose, green, white, and deep purple.

Stake the bloom stalk as it lengthens to prevent the weight of the flower from bending the stem. Once the bloom opens, cooler temperatures (about 65°F) prolong the bloom. The Maudiae hybrids are particularly dependable bloomers and excellent choices for the beginning grower. Paphs are usually 4 to 8 inches tall.

Phragmipediums (phrags) are closely related to paphiopedilums and share the same flower shape. Phragmipedium leaves are always green and more tightly upright, with foliage reaching 6 to 10 inches. Phrags produce bloom spikes up to 30 inches tall and multiple blooms on a single spike. Their flowers open in succession from the bottom up. Each flower lasts for several weeks, so a single spike can provide color for months.

Phragmipediums are terrestrial orchids and may be cool, intermediate, or warm growing, depending on the species or cultivar.

After watering, they should be allowed to sit in a saucer of water that is gradually absorbed by the potting medium. The saucer should be refilled if all of the water evaporates between waterings. Because phrags like to remain constantly moist, pot them in a nonporous container to slow evaporation.

Phragmipediums flower best in medium light from an east or west window. Their leaves turn dark green if they get too little light and yellow if they get too much. If light levels are not high enough, a plant may not flower, although its foliage may look healthy.

The more-frequent watering schedule leads to faster decomposition of the potting mix. As a result, phrags need repotting more frequently than many other orchids. They benefit from repotting every year, after flowering.

Paphiopedilum armeniacum

BLOOM: 3- to 4-inch diameter; yellow; inflated pouch with small red stripes at top; borne singly
GROWTH HABIT: Terrestrial; sympodial; mottled foliage
LIGHT REQUIREMENT: Medium
TEMPERATURE REQUIREMENT: Intermediate
ATTRIBUTES: Miniature

Paphiopedilum delenatii is a terrestrial orchid native to China and Vietnam. Its mottled foliage is an indication that it likes to grow in warm conditions.

Paphiopedilum delenatii 'Excel' × sib. 'Pink Balloon'

BLOOM: 4-inch diameter; pale pink; darker pink inflated pouch; 1 to 2 borne in succession
GROWTH HABIT: Terrestrial; sympodial; mottled foliage
LIGHT REQUIREMENT: Low
TEMPERATURE REQUIREMENT: Intermediate to warm
ATTRIBUTES: Fragrant; miniature

Paph. Dodge City 'High Noon' × Stefani Pitta 'Val'

BLOOM: 5-inch diameter; orange petals and pouch; white dorsal sepal with yellow and/or brown spots; borne singly
GROWTH HABIT: Terrestrial; sympodial; green foliage
LIGHT REQUIREMENT: Low
TEMPERATURE REQUIREMENT: Cool
ATTRIBUTES: Unusual shape and color combination

Paphiopedilum Hsinying Carlos

BLOOM: 4- to 5-inch diameter; dark pink with green markings and black warts; purple pouch; 1 to 2 borne in succession
GROWTH HABIT: Terrestrial; sympodial; mottled foliage
LIGHT REQUIREMENT: Low
TEMPERATURE REQUIREMENT: Cool to warm
ATTRIBUTES: Maudiae type; tolerates a wide temperature range

Paphiopedilum Hsinying Dragon

BLOOM: 4- to 6-inch diameter; green petals, yellow-green pouch; white dorsal sepal with green stripes; borne singly
GROWTH HABIT: Terrestrial; sympodial; mottled foliage
LIGHT REQUIREMENT: Low
TEMPERATURE REQUIREMENT: Intermediate to warm
ATTRIBUTES: Maudiae type; long-lasting bloom

Paphiopedilum
Limerick × Greenvale

BLOOM: 4- to 5-inch diameter; yellow with red
stripes and spots; white margins on dorsal sepal;
yellow pouch

GROWTH HABIT: Terrestrial; sympodial;
green foliage

LIGHT REQUIREMENT: Low

TEMPERATURE REQUIREMENT: Cool

ATTRIBUTES: Large, showy flower

Paphiopedilum lowii
'Magic Princess'

BLOOM: 5- to 7-inch diameter; green with maroon
stripes, dots, and pouch; very long petals have
broad, rounded pink tips; 1 to 6 per spike

GROWTH HABIT: Terrestrial; sympodial; green foliage

LIGHT REQUIREMENT: Medium

TEMPERATURE REQUIREMENT: Intermediate

ATTRIBUTES: Unusual flower color and shape; multiflowered spike

Paphiopedilum Maudiae

BLOOM: 3- to 5-inch diameter; maroon or white with
green accents; fringed, warty petals; large striped
dorsal sepal; sometimes multiflowered

GROWTH HABIT: Terrestrial; sympodial; mottled
foliage

LIGHT REQUIREMENT: Low

TEMPERATURE REQUIREMENT: Cool to warm

ATTRIBUTES: Long-lasting bloom

Paphiopedilum micranthum
'Weltz Deal'

BLOOM: 3-inch diameter; pink flushed with yellow;
maroon veins; inflated pink pouch; borne singly

GROWTH HABIT: Terrestrial; sympodial;
mottled foliage

LIGHT REQUIREMENT: Medium

TEMPERATURE REQUIREMENT: Warm

ATTRIBUTES: Miniature; unusual shape

Paphiopedilum primulinum

BLOOM: 3-inch diameter; fringed yellow petals; yellow pouch; yellow-green dorsal sepal; produces one flower after another

GROWTH HABIT: Lithophyte; sympodial; green foliage

LIGHT REQUIREMENT: Low to medium

TEMPERATURE REQUIREMENT: Intermediate to warm

ATTRIBUTES: Small plant; long bloom sequences; color varies within species

Paphiopedilum rothschildianum

BLOOM: 6- to 12-inch diameter; white petals with purple spots and stripes; pouch with maroon veins; 2 to 4 per spike open simultaneously

GROWTH HABIT: Terrestrial or lithophyte; sympodial; green foliage

LIGHT REQUIREMENT: Medium

TEMPERATURE REQUIREMENT: Warm to intermediate

ATTRIBUTES: Slow to reach blooming size

Paphiopedilum rothschildianum 'Jim Krull'

BLOOM: 6- to 12-inch diameter; white with purple stripes; maroon pouch; 2 to 4 per spike open simultaneously

GROWTH HABIT: Terrestrial or lithophyte; sympodial; green foliage

LIGHT REQUIREMENT: Medium

TEMPERATURE REQUIREMENT: Intermediate to warm

ATTRIBUTES: Easier to grow than straight species

Paphiopedilum villosum

BLOOM: 3- to 5-inch diameter; orange petals; yellow pouch; flared dorsal sepal; white to yellow with maroon spots; shiny flower; borne singly

GROWTH HABIT: Epiphyte or lithophyte; sympodial; green foliage

LIGHT REQUIREMENT: Medium

TEMPERATURE REQUIREMENT: Intermediate

ATTRIBUTES: Unusual color combination

Paphiopedilum wenshanense

BLOOM: 3-inch diameter; cream with dark purple spots; spotted extended pouch with yellow center; borne singly

GROWTH HABIT: Terrestrial; sympodial; mottled foliage

LIGHT REQUIREMENT: Low to medium

TEMPERATURE REQUIREMENT: Intermediate to warm

ATTRIBUTES: Miniature; unusual color; also sold as *P. conco-bellatulum* or *P. concobellatulum*

Paphiopedilum Winston Churchill

BLOOM: 4- to 5-inch diameter; white with dark pink veins or spots; cream pouch with red markings; borne singly

GROWTH HABIT: Terrestrial; sympodial; green foliage

LIGHT REQUIREMENT: Low

TEMPERATURE REQUIREMENT: Cool

ATTRIBUTES: Large flower; nice variety within grex

Phragmipedium besseae

BLOOM: 3-inch diameter; scarlet; pouch with pale yellow stripes; 1 to 3 per spike, opening sequentially

GROWTH HABIT: Terrestrial or lithophyte; sympodial

LIGHT REQUIREMENT: Low to medium

TEMPERATURE REQUIREMENT: Intermediate

ATTRIBUTES: Vibrant color; not the easiest for home growing

Phragmipedium Eric Young × Sorcerer's Apprentice

BLOOM: 4- to 6-inch diameter; red flushed with yellow; red pouch with yellow interior and red spots; 1 to 4 per spike, borne singly or in multiples

GROWTH HABIT: Terrestrial; sympodial

LIGHT REQUIREMENT: Medium

TEMPERATURE REQUIREMENT: Cool to intermediate

ATTRIBUTES: Showy color; long-lasting bloom; tall spikes; compare to *Phrag.* Sorcerer's Apprentice

Phragmipedium Fliquet

BLOOM: 3- to 4-inch diameter; 5-inch red petals with wavy margins; dorsal sepal cream with red veins; red pouch with cream interior and red spots; 1 to 4 per spike

GROWTH HABIT: Terrestrial; sympodial

LIGHT REQUIREMENT: Medium

TEMPERATURE REQUIREMENT: Cool to intermediate

ATTRIBUTES: Large flower with unusual shape, color, and pattern

Phragmipedium Grande

BLOOM: 3-inch diameter; 8 inches long; white petals streaked with green and red; dorsal sepal white with green veins; pink pouch with red spots; 1 to 4 per spike, borne simultaneously

GROWTH HABIT: Terrestrial; sympodial

LIGHT REQUIREMENT: Medium to high

TEMPERATURE REQUIREMENT: Cool to intermediate

ATTRIBUTES: Extra-long ornamental petals; intricate pattern

Phragmipedium schlimii 'Wilcox'

BLOOM: 2- to 3-inch diameter; white flushed with pink; dark pink inflated pouch flushed with yellow; 1 to 3 per spike, borne singly in sequence

GROWTH HABIT: Terrestrial or lithophyte; sympodial

LIGHT REQUIREMENT: Medium to high

TEMPERATURE REQUIREMENT: Intermediate to warm

ATTRIBUTES: Fragrant; miniature; long-lasting bloom

Phragmipedium Sorcerer's Apprentice

BLOOM: 4- to 6-inch diameter; yellow petals with red veins and wavy red margins; lip flushed with red; 1 to 6 per spike, borne in multiples

GROWTH HABIT: Terrestrial; sympodial

LIGHT REQUIREMENT: Medium

TEMPERATURE REQUIREMENT: Cool to intermediate

ATTRIBUTES: Showy bloom; tall spikes, long-lasting bloom

Dendrobium relatives

The genus *Dendrobium* is highly varied, containing some of the orchid world's most alluring flowers. Dendrobiums are sympodials that may be epiphytic, lithophytic, or terrestrial. Leaves may be thin or thick, leathery or papery. Pseudobulbs may be smooth or hairy, short or long, slim or plump. Flowers may grow upright or pendent, and plants grow best potted in bark mix or mounted on bark slabs.

No matter how different one dendrobium is from another, they all share at least one common characteristic: a spur formed by the fused base of the sepals.

Because individual dendrobiums vary so greatly from one another, it's impossible to give general cultural recommendations that are valid for the genus as a whole. However, the genus can be divided into sections that share growing requirements.

Phalaenopsis dendrobiums are named because their flowers resemble phalaenopsis flowers in shape (except for the fused sepals mentioned above). These are among the easiest dendrobiums for home growers. They are evergreen, warm growers, and require medium light to bloom.

They are drought-tolerant and grow with slim pseudobulbs shaped like spindles, also called canes. Generally these dendrobiums bloom in fall and winter, but if you force dormancy (giving them three to four weeks of cool, dry rest at about 55°F) after the first flowering, you may be able to force them into a second bloom cycle. Sizes vary from miniature to 3 feet tall.

They grow best when potbound. It's not unusual to see a 3-foot-tall dendrobium growing and flowering well in a 4-inch pot. To prevent the heavy top growth from tipping over, place the 4-inch pot inside a 6-inch pot for extra ballast.

Antelope dendrobiums are evergreen and well-suited to home growing. They are warm growers that bloom best in medium to high light. Their pseudobulbs are slim canes. The flowers of antelope dendrobiums (also called spatulate dendrobiums) have two twisted petals on top that resemble the horns of an antelope. Even without dormancy they may bloom more than once a year.

Nobile dendrobiums are irresistible but tricky to get into bloom. The orchid won't bloom unless you give it six to eight weeks of nighttime temperatures at about 50°F. Plants produce pairs of flowers on short stems along the top half of their canes. Blooms may be white, pink, yellow, orange, magenta, or lavender and are often fragrant. You can promote flowering by leaving nobile dendrobiums outdoors in fall, bringing them inside when nighttime temperatures approach 50°F. Some recent hybrids have been bred to bloom without the temperature drop.

Many other dendrobiums are deciduous, which can be confusing for the beginning grower. Foliage may precede flowering, then drop. Leaves and flowers may drop after the bloom fades as the orchids enter dormancy.

In either case, bare canes are not a cause for alarm. This is part of the plant's normal life cycle and signals that it's time to cut back on the water and fertilizer.

Deciduous dendrobiums may be cool, intermediate, or warm growing. In every case, during dormancy they should be kept on the cool side.

Dendrobium canes can grow anywhere from 2 to 48 inches tall or long, but most are in the 12- to 18-inch range.

DENDROBIUMS AT A GLANCE

TYPE: Sympodial, epiphyte
LIGHT: Medium to high
TEMP: Intermediate
MIX: Medium-grain bark mix or mounted on a slab

Dendrobium Burma Sunshine 'Blue' has flowers that vary from chocolate brown to purple with contrasting chartreuse and white hues.

Dendrobium
Ahulani Hinojosa

BLOOM: 3-inch diameter; deep rose with greenish-white center; deep rose lip, 5 to 20 per spike

GROWTH HABIT: Epiphyte; sympodial; cylindrical canes; evergreen

LIGHT REQUIREMENT: Medium to high

TEMPERATURE REQUIREMENT: Intermediate to warm

ATTRIBUTES: Phal type; long-lasting bloom

Dendrobium anosmum

BLOOM: 3- to 4-inch diameter; pinkish-purple; 1 to 2 blooms in clusters of flowers arranged on stem; 20 to 50 per stem

GROWTH HABIT: Epiphyte; sympodial; cylindrical canes; deciduous

LIGHT REQUIREMENT: Medium to high

TEMPERATURE REQUIREMENT: Intermediate to warm

ATTRIBUTES: A large plant; sometimes fragrant

Dendrobium antennatum
'Lemon Twist' × sibling

BLOOM: 1- to 2-inch diameter; twisted green sepals; white flower with purple stripes; 4 to 8 per spike

GROWTH HABIT: Epiphyte; sympodial; cylindrical canes; evergreen

LIGHT REQUIREMENT: Medium to high

TEMPERATURE REQUIREMENT: Intermediate to warm

ATTRIBUTES: Antelope type; unusual flower shape; fragrant; multiple spikes per plant

Dendrobium atroviolaceum

BLOOM: 2- to 2½-inch diameter; white with brown speckles; tubular lip with purple markings; 2 to 10 per spike

GROWTH HABIT: Epiphyte; sympodial; pseudobulbs; evergreen

LIGHT REQUIREMENT: Medium to high

TEMPERATURE REQUIREMENT: Intermediate to warm

ATTRIBUTES: Miniature; long-lasting bloom; fragrant

Dendrobium Aussie Aurora

BLOOM: 3-inch diameter; yellow; paler lip with red markings; shaped like stars; 6 to 12 per spike

GROWTH HABIT: Epiphyte; sympodial; cylindrical canes; evergreen

LIGHT REQUIREMENT: Medium to high

TEMPERATURE REQUIREMENT: Cool

ATTRIBUTES: Intricate markings; multiple spikes per plant

Dendrobium bullenianum

BLOOM: 1-inch diameter; orange striped with red; 20 to 40 tightly clustered on pendent canes

GROWTH HABIT: Epiphyte; sympodial; cylindrical canes; deciduous

LIGHT REQUIREMENT: High

TEMPERATURE REQUIREMENT: Warm

ATTRIBUTES: Showy bloom; interesting growth habit

Dendrobium Burana Angel 'Blue'

BLOOM: 2½-inch diameter; purple with white center; 5 to 15 per spike

GROWTH HABIT: Epiphyte; sympodial; cylindrical canes; evergreen

LIGHT REQUIREMENT: High

TEMPERATURE REQUIREMENT: Intermediate to warm

ATTRIBUTES: Phal type; long-lasting bloom

Dendrobium Burana Pink

BLOOM: 2½-inch diameter; magenta with white center; 5 to 15 per spike

GROWTH HABIT: Epiphyte; sympodial; cylindrical canes; evergreen

LIGHT REQUIREMENT: High

TEMPERATURE REQUIREMENT: Intermediate to warm

ATTRIBUTES: Phal type; long-lasting bloom

Dendrobium convolutum

BLOOM: 1½-inch diameter; yellow-green; shaped like stars; large purple lip and purple-striped center; 2 to 5 per spike

GROWTH HABIT: Epiphyte; sympodial; cylindrical canes; evergreen

LIGHT REQUIREMENT: Medium to high

TEMPERATURE REQUIREMENT: Warm

ATTRIBUTES: Miniature; interesting color combination; many flowers

Dendrobium cruentum × Suzukii

BLOOM: 1½- to 2½-inch diameter; cream-yellow; textured, large orange lip; 1 to 4 per plant

GROWTH HABIT: Epiphyte; sympodial; cylindrical canes; deciduous

LIGHT REQUIREMENT: High

TEMPERATURE REQUIREMENT: Warm

ATTRIBUTES: Unusual color combination, shape, and texture

Dendrobium cucullatum

BLOOM: 3-inch diameter; white flushed with lavender; lavender lip; 10 to 40 on bare stems, borne in groups of 1 to 2

GROWTH HABIT: Epiphyte; sympodial, cylindrical canes, deciduous

LIGHT REQUIREMENT: Medium to high

TEMPERATURE REQUIREMENT: Warm

ATTRIBUTES: Pendent bloom; long canes

Dendrobium cuthbertsonii

BLOOM: 2-inch diameter; vermilion flushed with yellow; lip edged in purple; many flowers, each borne singly

GROWTH HABIT: Epiphyte, lithophyte, or terrestrial; sympodial; small pseudobulbs; evergreen

LIGHT REQUIREMENT: Medium to high

TEMPERATURE REQUIREMENT: Cool to intermediate

ATTRIBUTES: Miniature; wide flower color variety; long-lasting bloom; warty foliage; challenging to grow

Dendrobium Doctor Uthai

BLOOM: 2- to 3-inch diameter; greenish-yellow sepals, white petals; purple lip striped with white; 5 to 15 per spike

GROWTH HABIT: Epiphyte; sympodial; cylindrical canes; evergreen

LIGHT REQUIREMENT: High

TEMPERATURE REQUIREMENT: Intermediate to warm

ATTRIBUTES: Antelope type; unusual flower shape

Dendrobium Emma 'Pink'

BLOOM: 2- to 3-inch diameter; white flushed with pale pink; magenta lip; 5 to 10 per spike

GROWTH HABIT: Epiphyte; sympodial; cylindrical canes; evergreen

LIGHT REQUIREMENT: High

TEMPERATURE REQUIREMENT: Intermediate to warm

ATTRIBUTES: Phal type; unusual, delicate color and pattern

Dendrobium Enobi Purple 'Splash'

BLOOM: 2- to 3-inch diameter; white brushed with purple along margins; lip brushed with purple; 5 to 10 per spike

GROWTH HABIT: Epiphyte; sympodial; cylindrical canes; evergreen

LIGHT REQUIREMENT: High

TEMPERATURE REQUIREMENT: Intermediate to warm

ATTRIBUTES: Phal type; beautiful markings

Dendrobium Fantasia

BLOOM: 2- to 3-inch diameter; purple-magenta with white center; ruffled petals and lip; lip white with yellow center and purple margin; 10 to 30 per plant, borne singly or in pairs on short stems

GROWTH HABIT: Epiphyte; sympodial; cylindrical canes; deciduous

LIGHT REQUIREMENT: High

TEMPERATURE REQUIREMENT: Cool to intermediate

ATTRIBUTES: Nobile type; showy flowers

Dendrobium Frosty Dawn

BLOOM: 2- to 3-inch diameter; cream; large orange lip; 6 to 20 per cane, borne singly or in pairs on short stems

GROWTH HABIT: Epiphyte; sympodial; cylindrical canes; deciduous

LIGHT REQUIREMENT: High

TEMPERATURE REQUIREMENT: Cool to intermediate

ATTRIBUTES: Nobile type; unusual color combination

Dendrobium gracilicaule

BLOOM: ½-inch diameter; pale yellow speckled with red; 5 to 30 per spike

GROWTH HABIT: Epiphyte or lithophyte; sympodial; cylindrical canes; a few evergreen leaves at tips of canes

LIGHT REQUIREMENT: High

TEMPERATURE REQUIREMENT: Intermediate

ATTRIBUTES: Fragrant; multiple long spikes per plant

Dendrobium Irma Febo 'Reina'

BLOOM: 3-inch diameter; white with pale pink veins and magenta center; 5 to 10 per spike

GROWTH HABIT: Epiphyte; sympodial; cylindrical canes; evergreen

LIGHT REQUIREMENT: High

TEMPERATURE REQUIREMENT: Intermediate to warm

ATTRIBUTES: Phal type; intricate, delicate pattern and color

Dendrobium jonesii

BLOOM: 1-inch diameter; white with petals and sepals curved inward; 10 to 40 per spike

GROWTH HABIT: Epiphyte or lithophyte; sympodial; cylindrical canes; evergreen

LIGHT REQUIREMENT: High

TEMPERATURE REQUIREMENT: Intermediate

ATTRIBUTES: Fragrant; multiple spikes per plant; sometimes sold as *D. ruppianum*; flowers mature from white to yellow

Dendrobium lindleyi

BLOOM: 1- to 1½-inch diameter; yellow with orange center; 10 to 25 per spike

GROWTH HABIT: Epiphyte; sympodial; pseudobulbs; evergreen

LIGHT REQUIREMENT: High

TEMPERATURE REQUIREMENT: Intermediate

ATTRIBUTES: Fragrant; pendent bloom spike; also known as *D. aggregatum*

Dendrobium Lorrie Mortimer 'Mini'

BLOOM: 1-inch diameter; white with greenish-white twisted sepals; magenta lip; 5 to 10 per spike

GROWTH HABIT: Epiphyte; sympodial; cylindrical canes, evergreen

LIGHT REQUIREMENT: Medium to high

TEMPERATURE REQUIREMENT: Warm

ATTRIBUTES: Miniature; antelope type; unusual flower

Dendrobium nobile

BLOOM: 3- to 4-inch diameter; white flushed with pale pink; ruffled petals and lip; lip white with yellow center and pale pink margin; 5 to 20 per plant, borne in groups of 2 to 4 on short stems

GROWTH HABIT: Epiphyte; sympodial; cylindrical canes; deciduous

LIGHT REQUIREMENT: High

TEMPERATURE REQUIREMENT: Cool to intermediate

ATTRIBUTES: Nobile type; fragrant; long-lasting bloom

Dendrobium nobile Sea Marian 'Snow King' #58

BLOOM: 3-inch diameter; white to pale pink; ruffled petals and lip; 10 to 20 per plant, borne singly or in pairs

GROWTH HABIT: Epiphyte; sympodial; slim canes; deciduous

LIGHT REQUIREMENT: High

TEMPERATURE REQUIREMENT: Cool to intermediate

ATTRIBUTES: Nobile type; fragrant; delicate coloring

Dendrobium speciosum

BLOOM: 1- to 2-inch diameter; pale yellow; white lip with purple speckles; 20 to 100 per spike

GROWTH HABIT: Lithophyte or epiphyte; sympodial; pseudobulbs; evergreen

LIGHT REQUIREMENT: High

TEMPERATURE REQUIREMENT: Cool to intermediate

ATTRIBUTES: Fragrant; many flowered

Dendrobium spectabile

BLOOM: 2- to 3½-inch diameter, greenish yellow and red; dramatically twisted sepals; 1 to 15 per spike

GROWTH HABIT: Epiphyte; sympodial; cylindrical canes; evergreen

LIGHT REQUIREMENT: Medium to high

TEMPERATURE REQUIREMENT: Warm

ATTRIBUTES: Unusual flower shape; long-lasting bloom

Dendrobium Thai Pixie

BLOOM: 1-inch diameter; white with greenish-white twisted sepals; magenta lip; 5 to 10 per spike

GROWTH HABIT: Epiphyte; sympodial; cylindrical canes; evergreen

LIGHT REQUIREMENT: Medium to high

TEMPERATURE REQUIREMENT: Cool to warm

ATTRIBUTES: Compact growth habit; antelope type

Dendrobium Waianae Charisma 'Lovely'

BLOOM: 2- to 3½-inch diameter; white splashed with magenta; lip splashed with magenta; 5 to 15 per spike

GROWTH HABIT: Epiphyte; sympodial; cylindrical canes; evergreen

LIGHT REQUIREMENT: High

TEMPERATURE REQUIREMENT: Intermediate to warm

ATTRIBUTES: Phal type; long-lasting bloom

Jewel orchid relatives

Members of this group are terrestrials that tolerate lower light levels than most other orchids described in this book. Jewel orchids are mainly grown for their extraordinary foliage, growing as compact rosettes averaging 4 to 8 inches tall. Their leaves are decorative; their flowers are generally small. They grow best potted in a soilless potting mix or long-grain sphagnum moss.

JEWEL ORCHIDS AT A GLANCE

TYPE: Terrestrial, creeping growth habit
LIGHT: Low
TEMP: Intermediate
MIX: Soilless mix or sphagnum moss

Ludisia discolor, the only species in its genus, is an intermediate- to warm-temperature orchid. Its dark green, almost black, velvety leaves have red markings, and its growth habit is wide and spreading.

The thick and fleshy stems store moisture. When potted, the stems and leaves cascade over the edge of the pot, making a dramatic display. *Lus. discolor* grows well in a north-facing window and blooms in fall and winter, bearing spikes of numerous small white flowers.

Each stem usually produces a bloom spike 6 to 8 inches tall. A large plant looks quite dramatic in flower.

Avoid letting the leaves of *Lus. discolor* get wet. Water on the leaves can cause white spots or streaks, which mar their beauty.

The genus *Macodes* is closely related to *Ludisia* and shares its creeping growth habit. Like *Ludisia, Macodes* should be watered carefully. Water drops on foliage can leave marks behind. To prevent this, you can fill the plant's saucer with water so it can be absorbed from below.

These intermediate- to warm-temperature orchids do best in low light. Stunning foliage is dark green with contrasting veins and a netted pattern that looks sharply etched. Small brownish flowers pale by comparison. *Macodes* grows best potted in shallow containers.

The leaves of *Stenorrhynchos speciosum* grow in a compact rosette spotted with white dots. This is one of the few jewel orchids that produces showy flowers. Bloom spikes are 18 to 36 inches tall with clusters of small, brilliant red bracts surrounding small white flowers. Blooms last four to six weeks. It grows in cool to intermediate temperatures and does best in low light.

Anoectochilus are intermediate- to warm-temperature orchids that perform best in low light. Like *Lus. discolor,* they have fleshy, moisture-retentive stems that spread horizontally. spindle-shape Stems root as they make contact with potting mix, making this orchid easy to propagate from cuttings.

Dark, almost black leaves grow in a loose rosette and are netted with markings in white, gold, or pink. The undersides of the leaves may be pink. Flowers are white, yellow, or pink and are held in 4- to 8-inch spikes. Some blooms are attractively fringed.

Anoectochilus chapaensis

BLOOM: ½- to 1-inch diameter; yellow; spikes to 6 inches tall
GROWTH HABIT: Terrestrial; sympodial
LIGHT REQUIREMENT: Low
TEMPERATURE REQUIREMENT: Intermediate to warm
ATTRIBUTES: Greenish-black foliage with red veins

Ludisia discolor

BLOOM: ¾-inch diameter; white with yellow centers; spikes to 8 inches tall

GROWTH HABIT: Terrestrial; sympodial

LIGHT REQUIREMENT: Low to medium

TEMPERATURE REQUIREMENT: Intermediate to warm

ATTRIBUTES: Greenish-black foliage with red veins

Ludisia discolor var. alba

BLOOM: ¾-inch diameter; white with yellow centers; spikes to 8 inches tall

GROWTH HABIT: Terrestrial; sympodial

LIGHT REQUIREMENT: Low to medium

TEMPERATURE REQUIREMENT: Intermediate to warm

ATTRIBUTES: Greenish-black foliage with white veins; rare

Macodes petola

BLOOM: ½-inch diameter; insignificant reddish-brown blooms with white center; spikes to 10 inches tall

GROWTH HABIT: Terrestrial; sympodial

LIGHT REQUIREMENT: Low to medium

TEMPERATURE REQUIREMENT: Cool to warm

ATTRIBUTES: Greenish-black foliage with striking gold to silver veins; requires high humidity; well suited to terrariums

Stenorrhynchos speciosum

BLOOM: ½-inch diameter; red bracts surrounding small white to pink flowers; bloom spike to 30 inches tall

GROWTH HABIT: Terrestrial or epiphyte; sympodial

LIGHT REQUIREMENT: Medium

TEMPERATURE REQUIREMENT: Cool to intermediate

ATTRIBUTES: Rosette of green foliage speckled with silver

Oncidium relatives

This alliance contains more genera than any other and offers wide variety. Most of these sympodial orchids are epiphytic with prominent pseudobulbs. Flowers, usually in yellows and browns, can last several months. Some are fragrant while others have no scent. Blooms can range from ½ inch to 9 inches wide. They're often called "dancing ladies" for their flower shape and the way they tremble in the air on long, slim stems.

ONCIDIUMS AT A GLANCE

TYPE: Sympodial, epiphyte
LIGHT: Medium to high
TEMP: Intermediate
MIX: Medium- to coarse-grain or mounted

Members of the oncidium alliance are generally medium- to high-light orchids that thrive in a southern or western window. They grow best in small pots, so it's not unusual to find a 4-inch pot holding a plant with a 3-foot flower stalk.

Oncidiums grow best potted in medium-grain bark mix or as mounted specimens. They are cool, intermediate, or warm growing, depending on the species. Other naturally occurring genera in the group include *Brassia, Psychopsis, Tolumnia, Miltonia,* and *Miltoniopsis.* These are frequently interbred, producing hybrids that combine the best characteristics of their parents.

Miltonia and *Miltoniopsis* were lumped together as *Miltonia* until the mid-1970s and many plants labeled as *Miltonia* are actually *Miltoniopsis.* Both may be called pansy orchids, although miltoniopsis flowers are more pansylike, with flat, open blooms and contrasting central masks. They are cool growers. Temperatures higher than 80°F will impede flowering.

Miltoniopsis grow best in medium light. A single leaf emerges from each small pseudobulb. Miltonia flowers are pointier, shaped more like stars, and often fragrant. They are intermediate-temperature orchids, grow best in medium light, and produce two leaves from each small pseudobulb. Both require more consistent moisture than most epiphytes and should be grown in a fine-grain bark mix. Flowers, often fragrant, last three to four weeks.

Brassias are known as spider orchids. Blooms can stretch 8 to 12 inches from tip to tip, and bloom spikes may extend 3 feet beyond the plant. Some brassias bloom twice a year. Their flowers last from four to eight weeks; many are wonderfully fragrant. Brassias bear beautiful markings, primarily gold or green with speckles and bands of purple or maroon. Most brassias are epiphytes with large pseudobulbs. They are medium-light, intermediate-temperature orchids that grow best in a medium-grain bark mix. They're often hybridized for their remarkable flower shape and size.

Until recently, the genus *Odonotoglossum* included cool-growing orchids with showy blooms that were frequently used in hybridizing.

Odontoglossum species are difficult to grow in the average home because they require cool nighttime temperatures of 50 to 55°F. Odontoglossums and the genus *Cochlioda* are now part of the *Oncidium* genus, although you may still see their names on plant tags and in catalogs. All intergeneric hybrids that include *Odontoglossum* and *Cochlioda* will be renamed in the near future.

Both *Tolumnia* and *Psychopsis* had been lumped into the genus *Oncidium,* but now are accepted as genera of their own.

As a rule, oncidium hybrids are easier to grow than most species because breeding selects for the best characteristics, including adaptability and ease of culture. Full-size members of the oncidium alliance generally reach 12 to 24 inches tall, not counting flower spikes. *Tolumnias, Howearas,* and *Rodrumnias* are miniatures.

Intergeneric hybrids

Although not comprehensive, this list includes more common hybrids.

ALICEARA: *Brassia × Miltonia × Oncidium*
BAKERARA: *Brassia × Miltonia × Odontoglossum × Oncidium*
BEALLARA: *Brassia × Cochlioda × Miltonia × Odontoglossum*
BRASSADA: *Ada × Brassia*
BRASSIDIUM: *Brassia × Oncidium*
BURRAGEARA: *Cochlioda × Miltonia × Odontoglossum × Oncidium*
CYRTOCIDIUM: *Cyrtochilum × Oncidium*
DEGARMOARA: *Brassia × Miltonia × Odontoglossum*
HOWEARA: *Leochilus × Oncidium × Rodriguezia*
MILTASSIA: *Brassia × Miltonia*
MILTONIDIUM: *Miltonia × Oncidium*
ODONTIODA: *Cochlioda × Odontoglossum*
ONCIDESA: *Gomesa × Oncidium*
ONCIDOPSIS: *Miltoniopsis × Oncidium*
ONCOSTELE: *Oncidium × Rhyncostele*
RODRUMNIA: *Rodriguezia × Tolumnia*
SANDERARA: *Brassia × Cochlioda × Odontoglossum*
VUYLSTEKEARA: *Cochlioda × Miltonia × Odontoglossum*
WILSONARA: *Cochlioda × Odontoglossum × Oncidium*

Oncidium Tiger Crow 'Golden Girl' is a hybrid that used to be classified as an *Odontocidium*.

Aliceara Clownish 'Cotton Candy'

BLOOM: 3-inch diameter; pink with white and maroon markings; white flared lip; 4 to 10 per spike

GROWTH HABIT: Epiphyte; sympodial; pseudobulbs

LIGHT REQUIREMENT: High

TEMPERATURE REQUIREMENT: Cool to intermediate

ATTRIBUTES: Unusual color combination

Aliceara Marfitch 'Howard's Dream'

BLOOM: 4- to 5-inch diameter; pink with complex red and white markings; white, ruffled lip; 4 to 10 per spike

GROWTH HABIT: Epiphyte; sympodial; pseudobulbs

LIGHT REQUIREMENT: Medium to high

TEMPERATURE REQUIREMENT: Cool to intermediate

ATTRIBUTES: Unusual pattern on petals; genus will change to *Aliceara*

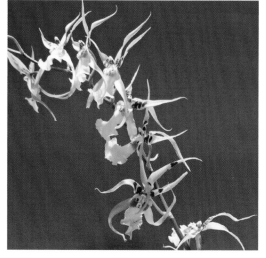

Aliceara Memoria Jay Yamada

BLOOM: 3- to 4-inch diameter; dark purple with yellow markings; light purple lip; 3 to 7 per spike

GROWTH HABIT: Epiphyte; sympodial; pseudobulbs

LIGHT REQUIREMENT: Medium to high

TEMPERATURE REQUIREMENT: Cool to warm

ATTRIBUTES: Fragrant; interesting color combination

Aliceara Pacific Nova 'Pacific Height'

BLOOM: 3- to 4-inch diameter; yellow with brown to red spots; 4 to 12 per spike

GROWTH HABIT: Epiphyte; sympodial; pseudobulbs

LIGHT REQUIREMENT: High

TEMPERATURE REQUIREMENT: Cool to warm

ATTRIBUTES: Large flowers shaped like spiders

Aliceara Patricia McCully 'Pacific Matriarch'

BLOOM: 4-inch diameter; pink with complex white and coral markings; white ruffled lip with yellow center; 4 to 10 per spike

GROWTH HABIT: Epiphyte; sympodial; pseudobulbs

LIGHT REQUIREMENT: Medium to low

TEMPERATURE REQUIREMENT: Cool

ATTRIBUTES: Fascinating pattern on flower petals

Brassia Memoria Bert Field 'Orange Prince'

BLOOM: 3- to 4-inch diameter; orange to yellow with brown markings; shaped like spiders; 5 to 12 per spike

GROWTH HABIT: Epiphyte; sympodial; pseudobulbs

LIGHT REQUIREMENT: Medium to high

TEMPERATURE REQUIREMENT: Cool to intermediate

ATTRIBUTES: Multiple spikes per plant

Brassia Rex 'Christine'

BLOOM: 6- to 7-inch diameter; pale yellow with brown markings; shaped like spiders; 10 to 15 per spike

GROWTH HABIT: Epiphyte; sympodial; large pseudobulbs

LIGHT REQUIREMENT: Medium to high

TEMPERATURE REQUIREMENT: Cool to warm

ATTRIBUTES: Fragrant; drought-tolerant; dramatic multiple spikes per plant

Brassidium FANGtastic Bob Henley

BLOOM: 4- to 5-inch diameter; pale yellow with brown markings; cream lip; shaped like spiders; curled petals; 10 to 18 per spike

GROWTH HABIT: Epiphyte; sympodial; pseudobulbs

LIGHT REQUIREMENT: Medium to high

TEMPERATURE REQUIREMENT: Cool to warm

ATTRIBUTES: Long-lasting bloom; extremely long bloom spike

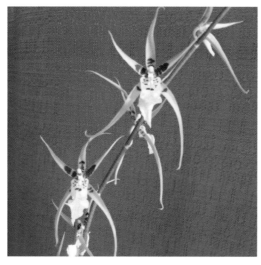

Brassidium
Gilded Urchin 'Ontario'

BLOOM: 6-inch diameter; pale yellow with brown
    markings; shaped like spiders; 5 to 18 per spike

GROWTH HABIT: Epiphyte; sympodial; pseudobulbs

LIGHT REQUIREMENT: High

TEMPERATURE REQUIREMENT: Cool to warm

ATTRIBUTES: Gentle fragrance; multiple
    bloom spikes per plant

Brassidium
Longlen 'Bill Switzer'

BLOOM: 3- to 4-inch diameter; greenish to yellow
    with brown markings; shaped like spiders;
    flared yellow lip; 5 to 15 per spike

GROWTH HABIT: Epiphyte; sympodial; pseudobulbs

LIGHT REQUIREMENT: Medium to high

TEMPERATURE REQUIREMENT: Cool to warm

ATTRIBUTES: Multiple spikes per plant

Brassidium White Knight

BLOOM: 4-inch diameter; brown with yellow
    markings; shaped like spiders; flared white lip; 5 to
    20 per spike

GROWTH HABIT: Epiphyte; sympodial; pseudobulbs

LIGHT REQUIREMENT: Medium to high

TEMPERATURE REQUIREMENT: Cool to warm

ATTRIBUTES: Branching bloom spike

Burrageara
Nelly Isler 'Swiss Beauty'

BLOOM: 3- to 4-inch diameter; orange-red;
    peach lip with orange speckles; yellow center;
    4 to 9 per spike

GROWTH HABIT: Epiphyte; sympodial; pseudobulbs

LIGHT REQUIREMENT: Medium to high

TEMPERATURE REQUIREMENT: Cool to
    intermediate

ATTRIBUTES: Fragrant; repeat bloom; multiple spikes
    per plant; genus will change to *Oncidopsis*

Cyrtocidium Gower Ramsey

BLOOM: 1- to 1½-inch diameter; yellow with brown
markings; large, ruffled yellow lip; 5 to 25 per
branching spike

GROWTH HABIT: Epiphyte; sympodial; pseudobulbs

LIGHT REQUIREMENT: Medium

TEMPERATURE REQUIREMENT: Intermediate
to warm

ATTRIBUTES: Classic "dancing lady" flower; the
cultivar 'Orange Delight' is especially attractive;
genus will change to *Oncidesa*

Degarmoara Winter Wonderland

BLOOM: 4- to 6-inch diameter; white with red to
brown markings at center; 3 to 6 per spike

GROWTH HABIT: Epiphyte; sympodial; pseudobulbs

LIGHT REQUIREMENT: Medium to high

TEMPERATURE REQUIREMENT: Cool
to intermediate

ATTRIBUTES: Fragrant; long-lasting bloom; genus will
change to *Aliceara*

Howeara Lava Burst 'Puanani'

BLOOM: 1-inch diameter; cupped; red with yellow
markings; 10 to 20 on branching spike

GROWTH HABIT: Epiphyte; sympodial; pseudobulbs

LIGHT REQUIREMENT: High

TEMPERATURE REQUIREMENT: Intermediate to
warm

ATTRIBUTES: Miniature; multiple spikes per plant

Miltassia Charles M. Fitch 'Izumi'

BLOOM: 4- to 5-inch diameter; pale green-purple
mottling; ruffled petals and lip with purple
margins; 3 to 6 per spike

GROWTH HABIT: Epiphyte; sympodial; pseudobulbs

LIGHT REQUIREMENT: High

TEMPERATURE REQUIREMENT: Cool to warm

ATTRIBUTES: Wild color combination and
pattern; long-lasting bloom; the genus will
change to *Bratonia*

Miltassia Kauai's Choice 'Tropical Fragrance'

BLOOM: 5- to 7-inch diameter; brown with yellow markings; white, ruffled lip; 4 to 15 per spike
GROWTH HABIT: Epiphyte; sympodial; pseudobulbs
LIGHT REQUIREMENT: High
TEMPERATURE REQUIREMENT: Cool to warm
ATTRIBUTES: Fragrant; multiple bloom spikes per plant; genus will change to *Bratonia*

Miltonia flavescens

BLOOM: 2- to 3-inch diameter; cream with red center; ruffled white lip; shaped like stars; 5 to 15 per spike
GROWTH HABIT: Epiphyte; sympodial; pseudobulbs
LIGHT REQUIREMENT: Medium
TEMPERATURE REQUIREMENT: Intermediate
ATTRIBUTES: Multiple long spikes per plant

Miltonidium Bartley Schwarz

BLOOM: 2-inch diameter; deep red; white-lobed lip; 5 to 20 per spike
GROWTH HABIT: Epiphyte; sympodial; pseudobulbs
LIGHT REQUIREMENT: Medium to high
TEMPERATURE REQUIREMENT: Cool to warm
ATTRIBUTES: Fragrant; multiple spikes per plant

Miltoniopsis Keiko Komoda

BLOOM: 4- to 5-inch diameter; red, cream, or white; lobed lip with white and maroon markings; 2 to 4 per spike
GROWTH HABIT: Epiphyte; sympodial; pseudobulbs
LIGHT REQUIREMENT: Medium to high
TEMPERATURE REQUIREMENT: Cool to intermediate
ATTRIBUTES: Velvety flower; highly variable within grex

Miltoniopsis phalaenopsis

BLOOM: 2- to 2½-inch diameter; white; lobed lip with purple and yellow markings; 3 to 5 per spike
GROWTH HABIT: Epiphyte; sympodial; pseudobulbs
LIGHT REQUIREMENT: Medium
TEMPERATURE REQUIREMENT: Intermediate
ATTRIBUTES: Multiple spikes per plant

Miltoniopsis roezlii

BLOOM: 3- to 3½-inch diameter; white sepals barely flushed with green; deep purple petals with white tips; large white lip with yellow center; 2 to 5 per spike
GROWTH HABIT: Epiphyte; sympodial; pseudobulbs
LIGHT REQUIREMENT: Medium
TEMPERATURE REQUIREMENT: Intermediate
ATTRIBUTES: Fragrant; interesting color combination

Miltoniopsis vexillaria

BLOOM: 3- to 4-inch diameter; white or pink or a combination of both; yellow center; 3 to 8 per spike
GROWTH HABIT: Epiphyte; sympodial; pseudobulbs
LIGHT REQUIREMENT: Medium
TEMPERATURE REQUIREMENT: Intermediate
ATTRIBUTES: Multiple spikes per plant; highly variable within grex

Oncidium George McMahon

BLOOM: 3-inch diameter; shades of yellow with pale orange and white markings; 5 to 12 per spike
GROWTH HABIT: Epiphyte; sympodial; pseudobulbs
LIGHT REQUIREMENT: Low to medium
TEMPERATURE REQUIREMENT: Cool
ATTRIBUTES: Blooms tightly clustered on stalk

Oncidium Jiuhbao Gold 'Tainan'

BLOOM: 1- to 3-inch diameter; yellow with red
to brown markings; large ruffled yellow lip;
10 to 40 per branching spike
GROWTH HABIT: Epiphyte; sympodial; pseudobulbs
LIGHT REQUIREMENT: Medium
TEMPERATURE REQUIREMENT: Cool to warm
ATTRIBUTES: Classic "dancing lady" flower; multiple
spikes per plant; genus will change to *Oncidesa*

Oncidium Kilauea 'TOW'

BLOOM: 2-inch diameter; orange with white tips;
white lip; 20 to 50 per branching spike
GROWTH HABIT: Epiphyte; sympodial; pseudobulbs
LIGHT REQUIREMENT: Medium
TEMPERATURE REQUIREMENT: Cool to warm
ATTRIBUTES: Multiple spikes per plant

Oncidium maculatum

BLOOM: 2-inch diameter; brown with green to yellow
markings; white lip; 5 to 20 per spike
GROWTH HABIT: Epiphyte; sympodial; pseudobulbs
LIGHT REQUIREMENT: Medium
TEMPERATURE REQUIREMENT: Intermediate
ATTRIBUTES: Multiple spikes per plant

Oncidium Pupukea Sunset

BLOOM: 1-inch diameter; yellow-green with large red
and cream lip; 10 to 50 per branching spike
GROWTH HABIT: Epiphyte; sympodial; pseudobulbs
LIGHT REQUIREMENT: Medium to high
TEMPERATURE REQUIREMENT: Cool to warm
ATTRIBUTES: Miniature; multiple spikes per plant

Oncidium Sharry Baby

BLOOM: 1½-inch diameter; branched spikes; 10 to 70 red-and-white flowers per spike

GROWTH HABIT: Epiphyte; sympodial; pseudobulbs

LIGHT REQUIREMENT: Medium

TEMPERATURE REQUIREMENT: Cool to warm

ATTRIBUTES: Strong fragrance; easy to grow

Oncidium Twinkle 'Fragrance Fantasy'

BLOOM: ½-inch diameter; white, pink, or red; branched spikes, 10 to 60 flowers per spike

GROWTH HABIT: Epiphyte; sympodial; pseudobulbs

LIGHT REQUIREMENT: Medium

TEMPERATURE REQUIREMENT: Cool to intermediate

ATTRIBUTES: Miniature; strong fragrance; multiple spikes per plant

Oncidopsis Pacific Paragon 'White Lightning'

BLOOM: 2- to 3-inch diameter; white with red markings; large, lobed lip; 10 to 30 per spike

GROWTH HABIT: Epiphyte; sympodial; pseudobulbs

LIGHT REQUIREMENT: Medium to high

TEMPERATURE REQUIREMENT: Cool to warm

ATTRIBUTES: Statuesque plant; also sold as *Miltonidium* Pacific Paragon 'White Lightning'

Oncostele Wildcat 'Golden Red Star'

BLOOM: 2- to 3-inch diameter; deep red with narrow yellow margins; 10 to 40 flowers per spike

GROWTH HABIT: Epiphyte; sympodial; pseudobulbs

LIGHT REQUIREMENT: Medium

TEMPERATURE REQUIREMENT: Cool to warm

ATTRIBUTES: Blooms more than once per year; branching bloom spike; multiple spikes per plant

Oncostele Wildcat 'Rainbow'

BLOOM: 2- to 3-inch diameter; deep red with yellow markings; yellow lip; 10 to 40 flowers per spike

GROWTH HABIT: Epiphyte; sympodial; pseudobulbs

LIGHT REQUIREMENT: Medium

TEMPERATURE REQUIREMENT: Cool to warm

ATTRIBUTES: Blooms more than once per year; branching bloom spike; multiple spikes per plant

Psychopsis Mariposa 'Alba'

BLOOM: 4-inch diameter; shades of yellow; shaped like butterflies; one flower at a time

GROWTH HABIT: Epiphyte; sympodial; pseudobulbs

LIGHT REQUIREMENT: Low to medium

TEMPERATURE REQUIREMENT: Intermediate to warm

ATTRIBUTES: Unusual flower shape; stem continues to produce one bloom at a time; long-lasting bloom

Psychopsis papilio 'Flying Wings'

BLOOM: 4- to 6-inch diameter; yellow-and-orange; shaped like butterflies; one flower at a time

GROWTH HABIT: Epiphyte; sympodial; pseudobulbs

LIGHT REQUIREMENT: Low to medium

TEMPERATURE REQUIREMENT: Intermediate to warm

ATTRIBUTES: Unusual flower shape; stem continues to produce one bloom at a time; long-lasting bloom

Rhynchostele cordata

BLOOM: 3-inch diameter; orange to red with yellow markings; white lip with red markings; shaped like stars; 5 to 12 per spike

GROWTH HABIT: Epiphyte; sympodial; pseudobulbs

LIGHT REQUIREMENT: Medium

TEMPERATURE REQUIREMENT: Cool

ATTRIBUTES: Multiple spikes per plant

Rodrumnia Francine Ontai × Rodrumnia Mystique

BLOOM: ½- to 1-inch diameter; deep pink with red spots; red-and-white center; 5 to 12 per spike

GROWTH HABIT: Epiphyte; sympodial; pseudobulbs

LIGHT REQUIREMENT: Medium to high

TEMPERATURE REQUIREMENT: Cool to intermediate

ATTRIBUTES: Miniature; lovely color combination and pattern

Sanderara Black Star 'Pacific Red Star'

BLOOM: 3- to 4-inch diameter; red with yellow markings; 5 to 15 per spike

GROWTH HABIT: Epiphyte; sympodial; pseudobulbs

LIGHT REQUIREMENT: Medium to high

TEMPERATURE REQUIREMENT: Cool to warm

ATTRIBUTES: Bright colors; intricate pattern; genus will change to *Brassidium*

Tolumnia Popoki 'Mitzi'

BLOOM: 1-inch diameter; deep rose flushed with pink or white; pink lobed lip; 5 to 12 per spike

GROWTH HABIT: Epiphyte; sympodial; pseudobulbs

LIGHT REQUIREMENT: Medium to high

TEMPERATURE REQUIREMENT: Cool to intermediate

ATTRIBUTES: Miniature; also sold as *Oncidium* Popoki 'Mitzii'

Vuylstekeara Fall in Love 'Lovely Lady'

BLOOM: 3- to 4-inch diameter; deep rose; pink lip with rose and yellow markings; 5 to 20 per spike

GROWTH HABIT: Epiphyte; sympodial; pseudobulbs

LIGHT REQUIREMENT: Medium

TEMPERATURE REQUIREMENT: Cool

ATTRIBUTES: Multiple bloom spikes per plant; repeat bloom; genus will change to *Miltonidium*

Wilsonara Castle Issa

BLOOM: 2- to 3-inch diameter; white with dark red blotches; lip flushed with yellow; 5 to 20 per spike
GROWTH HABIT: Epiphyte; sympodial; pseudobulbs
LIGHT REQUIREMENT: Medium
TEMPERATURE REQUIREMENT: Cool to warm
ATTRIBUTES: Gorgeous markings; also sold as *Burrageara* Castle Issa; genus will change to *Oncidium*

Wilsonara Linda Isler 'Red'

BLOOM: 3-inch diameter; clear red; ruffled lip has white margin; 3 to 25 per spike
GROWTH HABIT: Epiphyte; sympodial; pseudobulbs
LIGHT REQUIREMENT: Medium
TEMPERATURE REQUIREMENT: Cool to intermediate
ATTRIBUTES: Long-lasting bloom; also sold as *Vuylstekeara* Linda Isler 'Red'; genus will change to *Oncostele*

Wilsonara Sheila Anne

BLOOM: 3-inch diameter; red with coral and yellow markings; white lip with yellow flush; 6 to 20 per spike
GROWTH HABIT: Epiphyte; sympodial; pseudobulbs
LIGHT REQUIREMENT: Medium
TEMPERATURE REQUIREMENT: Cool
ATTRIBUTES: Unusual color combination and pattern; genus will change to *Oncidium*

Wilsonara Tigersette 'Wild Court'

BLOOM: 3- to 4-inch diameter; pale purple to pink with white and maroon markings; white lip; 4 to 20 per spike
GROWTH HABIT: Epiphyte; sympodial; pseudobulbs
LIGHT REQUIREMENT: Medium to high
TEMPERATURE REQUIREMENT: Cool to warm
ATTRIBUTES: Intricate pattern; multiple bloom spikes per plant; genus will change to *Oncidium*

Phalaenopsis relatives

Phalaenopsis orchids are the best-loved and easiest orchids for home growers. Their common name is moth orchid because the flowers look like moths hovering in the air. The flowers persist for months—the longest-lasting orchid blooms of all.

Phalaenopsis orchids (also called phals) are monopodial epiphytes. Most grow best in medium-grain bark mix, warm temperatures, and low to medium light. There are, however, some *Phalaenopsis* species that are cool to intermediate growers and these cannot be grown well under normal conditions. It's important to know what kind you have so you can meet your plant's special needs.

The genus *Doritis* is closely related to *Phalaenopsis*, causing the Kew World Monocot Checklist in 2001 to eliminate *Doritis* and include all former species in the genus *Phalaenopsis*. More time is needed to rename the many *Doritaenopsis* hybrids. That nothogenus will be phased out gradually, as renaming is accomplished.

Doritaenopsis is the intergeneric hybrid formed by crossing *Phalaenopsis* and *Doritis*. Although *Doritaenopsis* and *Phalaenopsis* are basically indistinguishable to the human eye, the *Doritis* ancestry contributes several significant characteristics. Doritis are terrestrial orchids and can be planted in a fine-grain bark mix. They are generally summer bloomers and their bloom spikes are often straight where phalaenopsis bloom spikes tend to arch. Doritis also contributes strong magenta color to the gene pool.

Members of the phalaenopsis alliance are available in a wide range of flower colors, including white, pink, yellow, orange, deep rose, and lavender. You can find striped and spotted hybrids.

Flowers may be flat and rounded or shaped like stars. Full-size flowers are 2 to 3 inches in diameter and are held on spikes that can grow 36 inches long, sometimes branching. Miniatures have flowers 1 to 1½ inches in diameter and bloom spikes 8 to 18 inches tall.

Foliage is usually dark green, but some leaves have lovely mottled patterns in gray or white margins. Foliage is succulent and straplike.

Phalaenopsis typically bloom once a year but can often be coaxed into a second round of bloom. When the last flower fades, if the bloom stalk is still green, cut it just above the third or fourth node and wait a few weeks. This may stimulate growth in a dormant bud and produce a second bloom stalk branching from below the cut.

These orchids are slow growers. Expect to see two or three new leaves annually. They need repotting once every year or two. Wait until your orchid has finished blooming to repot, and then do so only when the tips of the aerial roots are green. This indicates that the plant is in active growth.

Phalaenopsis and doritaenopsis orchids have foliage 4 to 8 inches tall, while mini-phal foliage can be 2 to 4 inches tall.

PHALAENOPSIS AT A GLANCE

TYPE: Monopodial, epiphyte
LIGHT: Low to medium
TEMP: Warm
MIX: Fine- to medium-grain

Doritaenopsis
Anna-Larati Soekardi

BLOOM: 1-inch diameter; reflexed white flower; white-and-magenta lip with yellow flush; 5 to 10 per spike
GROWTH HABIT: Epiphyte; monopodial
LIGHT REQUIREMENT: Low
TEMPERATURE REQUIREMENT: Intermediate to warm
ATTRIBUTES: Miniature; interesting flower shape

Doritaenopsis Leopard Prince 'M-P0450' will undoubtedly be renamed because its doritis parent is now classified as a phalaenopsis.

Doritaenopsis Brother Vanessa Hannay 'DeLeon #1'

BLOOM: 3- to 4- inch diameter; white with deep pink center; orange-and-yellow lip; 5 to 15 per spike
GROWTH HABIT: Epiphyte; monopodial
LIGHT REQUIREMENT: Low to medium
TEMPERATURE REQUIREMENT: Intermediate to warm
ATTRIBUTES: Striking color contrast

Doritaenopsis Chian Xen Pearl 'Ming Ho'

BLOOM: 3- to 4-inch diameter; white with maroon speckles; some pink flushing; maroon lip; 5 to 15 per spike
GROWTH HABIT: Epiphyte; monopodial
LIGHT REQUIREMENT: Low to medium
TEMPERATURE REQUIREMENT: Intermediate to warm
ATTRIBUTES: Intricate pattern on flower

Doritaenopsis Ever Spring Prince

BLOOM: 3- to 3½-inch diameter; deep rose with white margins; pink lip with white margins; 5 to 15 per branching spike
GROWTH HABIT: Epiphyte; monopodial
LIGHT REQUIREMENT: Low to medium
TEMPERATURE REQUIREMENT: Intermediate to warm
ATTRIBUTES: Dramatic color contrast

Doritaenopsis Fuller's Sunset

BLOOM: 3- to 4-inch diameter; yellow; orange lip; 5 to 15 per spike
GROWTH HABIT: Epiphyte; monopodial
LIGHT REQUIREMENT: Low to medium
TEMPERATURE REQUIREMENT: Intermediate to warm
ATTRIBUTES: Unusual color combination

Doritaenopsis I-Hsin Sesame

BLOOM: 4- to 4½-inch diameter; cream with dense, even pattern of pink spots; pink lip; 5 to 15 per spike

GROWTH HABIT: Epiphyte; monopodial

LIGHT REQUIREMENT: Low to medium

TEMPERATURE REQUIREMENT: Intermediate to warm

ATTRIBUTES: Large flowers; intricate pattern; may tolerate cool evening temperatures to 60°F

Doritaenopsis I-Hsin Sun Beauty

BLOOM: 3- to 4-inch diameter; white with pink spots concentrated at center; pink lip; 5 to 20 per spike

GROWTH HABIT: Epiphyte; monopodial

LIGHT REQUIREMENT: Low to medium

TEMPERATURE REQUIREMENT: Intermediate to warm

ATTRIBUTES: Large flowers; intricate pattern; may tolerate cool evening temperatures to 60°F

Doritaenopsis Kenneth Schubert

BLOOM: 1½-inch diameter; pale purple; dark purple lip; 5 to 15 per spike

GROWTH HABIT: Epiphyte; monopodial

LIGHT REQUIREMENT: Low

TEMPERATURE REQUIREMENT: Intermediate to warm

ATTRIBUTES: Rare color combination; miniature

Doritaenopsis Leopard Prince

BLOOM: 3- to 4-inch diameter; white with pink spots, concentrated at center; pink-and-white lip with yellow markings; 5 to 20 per spike

GROWTH HABIT: Epiphyte; monopodial

LIGHT REQUIREMENT: Low to medium

TEMPERATURE REQUIREMENT: Intermediate to warm

ATTRIBUTES: Large flowers; intricate pattern; may tolerate cool evening temperatures to 60°F

Doritaenopsis
Shawangunk Sunset

BLOOM: 3-inch diameter; dusky rose with yellow margins; yellow-and-white lip with maroon speckles; 5 to 15 per spike

GROWTH HABIT: Epiphyte; monopodial

LIGHT REQUIREMENT: Low to medium

TEMPERATURE REQUIREMENT: Intermediate to warm

ATTRIBUTES: Colors reminiscent of a sunset; may tolerate cool evening temperatures to 60°F

Doritaenopsis
Sogo Chabstic 'A09533'

BLOOM: 1½-inch diameter; white flower with deep rose center; magenta lip; 5 to 10 per spike

GROWTH HABIT: Epiphyte; monopodial

LIGHT REQUIREMENT: Low

TEMPERATURE REQUIREMENT: Intermediate to warm

ATTRIBUTES: Miniature; delicate flower; multiple branching spikes per plant

Doritaenopsis
Taida Sweetheart '#8'

BLOOM: 3- to 4-inch diameter; cream with pink flush; magenta lip with yellow markings; 5 to 15 per spike

GROWTH HABIT: Epiphyte; monopodial

LIGHT REQUIREMENT: Low to medium

TEMPERATURE REQUIREMENT: Intermediate to warm

ATTRIBUTES: Delicate coloring; older plants produce branching spikes

Doritaenopsis
Taisuco Firebird

BLOOM: 3- to 4-inch diameter; white with magenta edging and pink veins; magenta lip and yellow markings; 5 to 10 per spike

GROWTH HABIT: Epiphyte; monopodial

LIGHT REQUIREMENT: Low to medium

TEMPERATURE REQUIREMENT: Intermediate to warm

ATTRIBUTES: Intricate pattern

Doritaenopsis Tiannong Glory

BLOOM: 3- to 4-inch diameter; white with magenta edging and pink veins; magenta lip with yellow markings; 5 to 10 per spike

GROWTH HABIT: Epiphyte; monopodial

LIGHT REQUIREMENT: Low to medium

TEMPERATURE REQUIREMENT: Intermediate to warm

ATTRIBUTES: Intricate pattern

Doritaenopsis Tinny Honey

BLOOM: 4- to 5-inch diameter; white flushed with pink; pink veins; maroon lip with yellow markings; 5 to 25 per spike

GROWTH HABIT: Epiphyte; monopodial

LIGHT REQUIREMENT: Low to medium

TEMPERATURE REQUIREMENT: Intermediate to warm

ATTRIBUTES: Large flowers; interesting combination of pastel and saturated colors

Doritaenopsis Yu Pin Dream Girl

BLOOM: 3- to 4-inch diameter; pink-flushed white with pink spots and maroon streaks, and spots at tips; magenta lip; 5 to 10 per spike

GROWTH HABIT: Epiphyte; monopodial

LIGHT REQUIREMENT: Low to medium

TEMPERATURE REQUIREMENT: Intermediate to warm

ATTRIBUTES: Flashy pattern and color combination; may tolerate evening temperatures to 60°F

Phalaenopsis amabilis

BLOOM: 4- to 4½-inch diameter; white sometimes flushed with pale pink; white lip flushed with yellow; 5 to 15 per spike

GROWTH HABIT: Epiphyte; monopodial

LIGHT REQUIREMENT: Low to medium

TEMPERATURE REQUIREMENT: Intermediate to warm

ATTRIBUTES: Fragrant; multiple spikes per plant; may tolerate evening temperatures to 60°F

Phalaenopsis amboinensis 'Potilean'

BLOOM: 2- to 2½-inch diameter; yellow with maroon stripes; maroon-and-white lip; 3 to 5 per spike

GROWTH HABIT: Epiphyte; monopodial

LIGHT REQUIREMENT: Low to medium

TEMPERATURE REQUIREMENT: Intermediate to warm

ATTRIBUTES: Fragrant; multiple spikes per plant; spikes produce blooms for several years, 1 to 2 at a time

Phalaenopsis Baldan's Kaleidoscope 'Golden Treasure'

BLOOM: 3- to 4-inch diameter; apricot with pink veins; magenta lip; 5 to 15 per branching spike

GROWTH HABIT: Epiphyte; monopodial

LIGHT REQUIREMENT: Low to medium

TEMPERATURE REQUIREMENT: Intermediate to warm

ATTRIBUTES: Outstanding color combination

Phalaenopsis Brother Little Heart

BLOOM: 2- to 3-inch diameter; white flushed slightly with magenta; magenta-and-white lip with yellow markings; 5 to 25 per spike

GROWTH HABIT: Epiphyte; monopodial

LIGHT REQUIREMENT: Low to medium

TEMPERATURE REQUIREMENT: Intermediate to warm

ATTRIBUTES: Unusual markings; size between miniature and standard

Phalaenopsis Brother Passat × Dtps. Brother Love Rosa

BLOOM: 3-inch diameter; dark purple with white tips and center; 5 to 8 per spike

GROWTH HABIT: Epiphyte; monopodial

LIGHT REQUIREMENT: Low to medium

TEMPERATURE REQUIREMENT: Intermediate to warm

ATTRIBUTES: Unusual color

Phalaenopsis cornu-cervi

BLOOM: 1½- to 2-inch diameter; greenish-yellow with small red speckles; white-and-yellow lip; 3 to 10 per spike

GROWTH HABIT: Epiphyte; monopodial

LIGHT REQUIREMENT: Low to medium

TEMPERATURE REQUIREMENT: Warm

ATTRIBUTES: Miniature; bloom spike resembles wavy rickrack ribbon; spikes produce blooms for several years, 1 to 2 at a time

Phalaenopsis Double Delight

BLOOM: 3- to 4-inch diameter; cream with pink veins and speckles; maroon lip with yellow markings; 5 to 15 per spike

GROWTH HABIT: Epiphyte; monopodial

LIGHT REQUIREMENT: Low to medium

TEMPERATURE REQUIREMENT: Intermediate to warm

ATTRIBUTES: Intricate pattern; rich colors

Phalaenopsis fasciata

BLOOM: 2-inch diameter; yellow with slight orange stripes; long, slim white lip; 3 to 5 blooms per spike

GROWTH HABIT: Epiphyte; monopodial

LIGHT REQUIREMENT: Low

TEMPERATURE REQUIREMENT: Intermediate to warm

ATTRIBUTES: Fragrant; multiple spikes per plant; spikes produce blooms for several years, 1 to 2 at a time

Phalaenopsis Fortune Buddha × Cassandra

BLOOM: 2- to 3-inch diameter; deep rose with narrow yellow margin and white center; deep rose-and-yellow lip; 5 to 15 blooms per spike

GROWTH HABIT: Epiphyte; monopodial

LIGHT REQUIREMENT: Low

TEMPERATURE REQUIREMENT: Intermediate to warm

ATTRIBUTES: Rich colors, may tolerate evening temperatures to 60°F

Phalaenopsis gigantea

BLOOM: 2- to 2½-inch diameter; white striped
with maroon or pink; white lip;
5 to 20 per spike; fragrant
GROWTH HABIT: Epiphyte; monopodial
LIGHT REQUIREMENT: Low
TEMPERATURE REQUIREMENT: Intermediate
ATTRIBUTES: Giant leaves; penny (pictured) gives
perspective on the size

Phalaenopsis Gold Tris 'SW'

BLOOM: 2- to 2½-inch diameter; pale yellow flushed
with pink at center; lip pink, yellow, and white;
5 to 30 per spike
GROWTH HABIT: Epiphyte; monopodial
LIGHT REQUIREMENT: Low
TEMPERATURE REQUIREMENT: Intermediate to
warm
ATTRIBUTES: Unusual color combination;
many-flowered bloom spike

Phalaenopsis Haur Jin Diamond 'Haur Jin'

BLOOM: 2- to 3-inch diameter; greenish-yellow with
maroon blotches; lip white, maroon, and yellow;
5 to 10 per spike
GROWTH HABIT: Epiphyte; monopodial
LIGHT REQUIREMENT: Low
TEMPERATURE REQUIREMENT: Intermediate to
warm
ATTRIBUTES: Flashy color combination

Phalaenopsis Little Emperor

BLOOM: 2- to 3-inch diameter; apricot sepals;
petals flushed with yellow; orange-and-yellow lip;
5 to 12 per spike
GROWTH HABIT: Epiphyte; monopodial
LIGHT REQUIREMENT: Low
TEMPERATURE REQUIREMENT: Intermediate to
warm
ATTRIBUTES: Unusual color combination; flower may
be semipeloric, showing deviations from normal
petals and sepals (pictured); petals mimic the lip
in color and texture

Phalaenopsis Malibu Madonna

BLOOM: 3-inch diameter; magenta; cream lip with maroon center; 5 to 10 per spike

GROWTH HABIT: Epiphyte; monopodial

LIGHT REQUIREMENT: Low to medium

TEMPERATURE REQUIREMENT: Intermediate to warm

ATTRIBUTES: Rich, highly contrasting colors; may tolerate evening temperatures to 60°F

Phalaenopsis pulcherrima var. *champornensis* 'Lakeview Yellow Splash'

BLOOM: 1-inch diameter; white with pink-and-yellow markings; white-and-yellow lip; 10 to 20 per spike

GROWTH HABIT: Epiphyte; monopodial

LIGHT REQUIREMENT: Low to medium

TEMPERATURE REQUIREMENT: Intermediate to warm

ATTRIBUTES: Miniature; unusual tricolor combination; also sold as *Doritis pulcherrima*

Phalaenopsis schilleriana

BLOOM: 2- to 3-inch diameter; pale pink flushed with darker pink; cream lip with orange-and-yellow markings; 5 to 35 per spike

GROWTH HABIT: Epiphyte; monopodial

LIGHT REQUIREMENT: Low to medium

TEMPERATURE REQUIREMENT: Intermediate to warm

ATTRIBUTES: Foliage with silver mottling; lightly fragrant; the more flowers produced, the smaller the flowers

Phalaenopsis Sogo Cake 'Orchis'

BLOOM: 2- to 3-inch diameter; yellow flecked with red; red flush on bottom sepals; white center; white-and-red lip; 10 to 20 on branching spikes

GROWTH HABIT: Epiphyte; monopodial

LIGHT REQUIREMENT: Low to medium

TEMPERATURE REQUIREMENT: Intermediate to warm

ATTRIBUTES: Unusual color combination and pattern; may tolerate evening temperatures to 60°F; multiple spikes per plant

Phalaenopsis stuartiana

BLOOM: 2- to 4-inch diameter; white with maroon speckles; white-and-maroon lip flushed with yellow; 10 to 40 per branching spike

GROWTH HABIT: Epiphyte; monopodial

LIGHT REQUIREMENT: Low to medium

TEMPERATURE REQUIREMENT: Intermediate to warm

ATTRIBUTES: Fragrant; unusual flower shape; the more flowers produced, the smaller the flowers

Phalaenopsis Taida King's Caroline

BLOOM: 2- to 2½-inch diameter; cream with magenta stripes; magenta-and-white lip; 5 to 12 per spike

GROWTH HABIT: Epiphyte; monopodial

LIGHT REQUIREMENT: Low

TEMPERATURE REQUIREMENT: Intermediate to warm

ATTRIBUTES: Striking pattern

Phalaenopsis Taida Mini Dog

BLOOM: 2- to 3-inch diameter; white flushed with pink; magenta lip; 10 to 15 per spike

GROWTH HABIT: Epiphyte; monopodial

LIGHT REQUIREMENT: Low to medium

TEMPERATURE REQUIREMENT: Intermediate to warm

ATTRIBUTES: Delicate, candy cane colors; size between miniature and standard

Phalaenopsis venosa 'Red Mahogany'

BLOOM: 1½- to 2-inch diameter; burnt orange with green to yellow margins and white center; white lip; 3 to 5 per spike

GROWTH HABIT: Epiphyte; monopodial

LIGHT REQUIREMENT: Low to medium

TEMPERATURE REQUIREMENT: Warm

ATTRIBUTES: Multiple spikes per plant; fragrant

Pleurothallis relatives

Members of the pleurothallis alliance are called pleurothallids. The most popular are compact plants that fit easily into small spaces in your house. Some of the flowers are so tiny you need a magnifying glass to fully appreciate their exquisite detail. These orchids grow well under fluorescent tubes.

PLEUROTHALLIS AT A GLANCE

TYPE: Sympodial, epiphyte
LIGHT: Low to medium
TEMP: Warm
MIX: Fine- to medium-grain

Masdevallias are the most popular members of this alliance, but they aren't the easiest orchids to grow. Most species are native to the cloud forests of the high Andes. This is reflected in their cultural requirements: They need cool temperatures, high humidity, and low to medium light.

Flowers are large compared with plant size and unusually shaped, with fused sepals that terminate in three tails. They come in a wide range of saturated colors. Masdevallias do not have pseudobulbs and are not drought-tolerant. They should be grown on dry wells in the same type of light appropriate for phalaenopsis and paphiopedilums. These sympodial, epiphytic orchids are often miniatures, ranging from 3 to 12 inches tall.

Most *Masdevallia* species grow in cool temperatures, with a few that prefer intermediate temperatures, and even fewer that tolerate warm temperatures. To grow them well, it's essential to know which kind you have. Hybridization focuses on combining the rich colors of the cool-growing species with the heat tolerance of less showy plants. As a result, you can find hybrid masdevallias that grow well in the average home when given adequate humidity. All should be potted in a fine-grain bark mix.

The genus *Pleurothallis* is large and varied, but most orchids grown by hobbyists are small and epiphytic. Flowers are small and unusually shaped, often growing from the center of a leaf. They also require high humidity and low to medium light but tolerate a wider range of temperatures. Pleurothallis also do not have pseudobulbs, and so need frequent watering. Some pleurothallis grow well as mounted specimens, and others should be grown in a fine-grain bark mix. They can be miniature to large; they are highly variable.

Taxonomists have recently moved many *Pleurothallis* orchids into several different genera, including *Specklinia* and *Stelis*. Many more divisions have been proposed for groups within this giant genus; it is a highly diverse group.

Specklinias are small plants, generally less than 8 inches tall.

It's crucial to get the moisture levels right for pleurothallids. Their high humidity requirements can be met by growing them on dry wells or in terrariums. These petite orchids are perfect candidates for growing in a closed case, where humidity levels can be closely controlled.

Avoid compensating for low humidity with extra watering. While pleurothallids require frequent watering due to their lack of pseudobulbs, overwatering can lead to root rot. A fast-draining medium is essential.

Masdevallia caesia

BLOOM: 3- to 6-inch length; yellow with reddish-brown center; 3-point bloom; long tails; borne singly on pendent stems
GROWTH HABIT: Epiphyte; sympodial
LIGHT REQUIREMENT: Low to medium
TEMPERATURE REQUIREMENT: Cool
ATTRIBUTES: Several flowers borne simultaneously; interesting hanging growth habit; blue-green leaves

Masdevallia decumana

BLOOM: 1½- to 3½-inch diameter; yellow with purple
    speckles; 3-point bloom; long tails; borne singly
    below foliage
GROWTH HABIT: Epiphyte; sympodial
LIGHT REQUIREMENT: Low to medium
TEMPERATURE REQUIREMENT: Cool
    to intermediate
ATTRIBUTES: Several flowers borne simultaneously;
    repeat bloom; unusual flower shape

Masdevallia veitchiana

BLOOM: 4- to 6-inch diameter; brilliant vermilion;
    3-point flower; borne singly
GROWTH HABIT: Terrestrial, lithophyte, or epiphyte;
    sympodial
LIGHT REQUIREMENT: Medium
TEMPERATURE REQUIREMENT: Cool
ATTRIBUTES: Outstanding flower color and shape;
    multiple blooms; long-lasting bloom

Pleurothallis allenii

BLOOM: ½- to 1-inch diameter; maroon with yellow
    edges; borne singly
GROWTH HABIT: Epiphyte; sympodial
LIGHT REQUIREMENT: Medium
TEMPERATURE REQUIREMENT: Intermediate
ATTRIBUTES: Repeat bloom; miniature;
    easy to bloom

Specklinia tribuloides

BLOOM: ½-inch diameter; bright vermilion; fleshy;
    shaped like claws; 1 to 4 per spike; flowers held at
    base of foliage
GROWTH HABIT: Epiphyte; sympodial
LIGHT REQUIREMENT: Low to medium
TEMPERATURE REQUIREMENT: Intermediate
ATTRIBUTES: Miniature; easy to grow; unusual flower
    shape; sometimes sold as *Pleurothallis tribuloides*

Vanda relatives

Vandas have a reputation for being difficult to grow, but depending on where you live, this isn't necessarily so. Vandas are warm-temperature, high-light orchids, making them an excellent choice for orchid hobbyists with greenhouses or gardeners who live in tropical and subtropical climates.

VANDAS AT A GLANCE

TYPE: Monopodial, epiphyte
LIGHT: Medium to high
TEMP: Usually intermediate to warm
MIX: Medium- to coarse-grain or mounted

Vandas are monopodial, epiphytic orchids and are often grown in open, slatted baskets that allow orchid roots to be completely exposed to the air. They also thrive in a coarse-grain bark mix. Vanda flowers are large, flat, and colorful. The plants can grow to be quite large, with foliage several feet tall and bloom spikes extending 24 inches or longer.

The genus *Euanthe* is very closely related to *Vanda*. It contains only one plant: *Eua. sanderiana*, which is often used in hybridization.

Ascocentrum orchids are frequently hybridized with *Vandas* to produce *Ascocendas*. Both ascocentrums and ascoscendas have cultural requirements similar to vandas, but they're slightly more adaptable and will tolerate medium light and intermediate temperatures. They are also both smaller than vandas.

Vandopsis orchids are intermediate to warm growers and prefer high light. They are quite large; some produce bloom spikes up to 6 feet long.

Aerangis and *Angraecum* (once lumped together into a single genus) grow best in intermediate to warm temperatures and a range of light intensities. Both are monopodial epiphytes and can be either bark-mounted or potted in a medium-grain bark mix. Flowers are predominantly white and many are fragrant.

Neofinetia orchids are also monopodial epiphytes and also produce fragrant, pale-colored flowers. However, they are cool- to intermediate-growing orchids and grow best in medium light. Some neofinetias have variegated foliage that makes them attractive even when they're not in bloom.

Rhynchostylis (known as the foxtail orchid) produces large clusters of flowers that resemble hyacinths in shape and come in many colors.

They are warm growing, medium- to high-light orchids and monopodial epiphytes. Grow them in baskets like vandas or mounted on slabs. *Rhynchovanda*, a hybrid of *Rhynchostylis* and *Vanda*, shares the cultural needs of its parents.

One of the smallest members of the vanda alliance is the genus *Haraella*. A monopodial epiphytic miniature with fragrant flowers smaller than a dime, it grows best as a mounted specimen. Haraellas flourish in medium light and intermediate temperatures.

Most vandaceous orchids are large, ranging from 8 to 36 inches tall. Miniatures include *Ascocenda*, *Ascocentrum*, *Haraella*, *Neofinetia*, and *Aerangis*.

Aerangis fastuosa

BLOOM: 1½- to 2½-inch diameter; brilliant white with long, curled spur at back of flower; 1 to 6 per spike
GROWTH HABIT: Epiphyte; monopodial
LIGHT REQUIREMENT: Medium
TEMPERATURE REQUIREMENT: Intermediate
ATTRIBUTES: Long-lasting bloom; fragrant; miniature

Aeridovanda Blue Spur

BLOOM: 2- to 3-inch diameter; pale purple; dark purple lip; 5 to 25 per spike
GROWTH HABIT: Epiphyte; monopodial
LIGHT REQUIREMENT: High
TEMPERATURE REQUIREMENT: Cool to warm
ATTRIBUTES: Fragrant

Angraecum eburneum

BLOOM: 2- to 3-inch diameter; green-and-white with long rear spur; 5 to 30 per spike
GROWTH HABIT: Epiphyte; monopodial
LIGHT REQUIREMENT: Medium
TEMPERATURE REQUIREMENT: Warm
ATTRIBUTES: Fragrant; large, sprawling growth habit

Ascocenda John De Biase 'Denise'

BLOOM: 3-inch diameter; purple or pink; 5 to 20 per spike
GROWTH HABIT: Epiphyte; monopodial
LIGHT REQUIREMENT: High
TEMPERATURE REQUIREMENT: Intermediate to warm
ATTRIBUTES: Multiple spikes per plant

Ascocenda Su-Fun Beauty 'Orange Belle'

BLOOM: 2-inch diameter; orange; 5 to 20 per spike
GROWTH HABIT: Epiphyte; monopodial
LIGHT REQUIREMENT: High
TEMPERATURE REQUIREMENT: Intermediate to warm
ATTRIBUTES: Repeat bloom; multiple spikes per plant

Ascocenda Yip Sum Wah 'Flame'

BLOOM: 2-inch diameter; coral to pink with darker netting; 5 to 25 per spike
GROWTH HABIT: Epiphyte; monopodial
LIGHT REQUIREMENT: High
TEMPERATURE REQUIREMENT: Intermediate to warm
ATTRIBUTES: Multiple, branching bloom spikes on mature plants

Ascocentrum ampullaceum

BLOOM: ½- to 1-inch diameter; pink, purple, or orange; 10 to 40 per spike
GROWTH HABIT: Epiphyte; monopodial
LIGHT REQUIREMENT: Medium to high
TEMPERATURE REQUIREMENT: Intermediate to warm
ATTRIBUTES: Several spikes per plant; dwarf

Ascocentrum miniatum

BLOOM: ½-inch diameter; orange or reddish-orange; 10 to 30 per spike
GROWTH HABIT: Epiphyte; monopodial
LIGHT REQUIREMENT: Medium to high
TEMPERATURE REQUIREMENT: Warm
ATTRIBUTES: Numerous spikes per plant

Ascocentrum Sagarik Gold

BLOOM: ½-inch diameter; rich orange; 10 to 30 per spike
GROWTH HABIT: Epiphyte, monopodial
LIGHT REQUIREMENT: High
TEMPERATURE REQUIREMENT: Intermediate to warm
ATTRIBUTES: Multiple bloom spikes on mature plants

Euanthe sanderiana var. alba

BLOOM: 3- to 5-inch diameter; white; bottom sepals flushed with yellowish-green; 5 to 10 per spike
GROWTH HABIT: Epiphyte; monopodial
LIGHT REQUIREMENT: High
TEMPERATURE REQUIREMENT: Warm
ATTRIBUTES: Fragrant; long-lasting bloom; sometimes sold as *Vanda sanderiana* var. *alba*

Haraella retrocalla

BLOOM: ½- to ¾-inch; yellow; fringed lip with purple splotch; fringe sometimes white; 1 to 4 per spike
GROWTH HABIT: Epiphyte; monopodial
LIGHT REQUIREMENT: Medium to high
TEMPERATURE REQUIREMENT: Intermediate
ATTRIBUTES: Fragrant; miniature; sometimes sold as *Haraella odorata*; repeat bloom; requires good air circulation

Neofinetia falcata

BLOOM: 1-inch diameter; white; curved petals and sepals; 3-inch spur; 2 to 10 per spike
GROWTH HABIT: Epiphyte or lithophyte; monopodial
LIGHT REQUIREMENT: Medium to high
TEMPERATURE REQUIREMENT: Intermediate to warm
ATTRIBUTES: Fragrant; miniature; long-lasting bloom

Renanthera monachica

BLOOM: 1½-inch diameter; yellow-orange with red spots; shaped like stars; as many as 50 per spike
GROWTH HABIT: Epiphyte; monopodial
LIGHT REQUIREMENT: High
TEMPERATURE REQUIREMENT: Warm
ATTRIBUTES: Outstanding bloom color and number; pendent, branching bloom spike; long-lasting bloom; requires high humidity

Rhynchostylis gigantea

BLOOM: 1- to 1½-inch diameter; pink, purple, red, or orange; highly variable markings include spots, blushes, and contrasting lips; 10 to 50 blooms per spike
GROWTH HABIT: Epiphyte; monopodial
LIGHT REQUIREMENT: High
TEMPERATURE REQUIREMENT: Warm
ATTRIBUTES: Strong fragrance; requires high humidity and good air circulation; multiple spikes produced by established plants

Rhynchostylis gigantea var. *alba*

BLOOM: 1- to 1½-inch diameter; white; 10 to 50 blooms per spike
GROWTH HABIT: Epiphyte; monopodial
LIGHT REQUIREMENT: High
TEMPERATURE REQUIREMENT: Warm
ATTRIBUTES: Strong fragrance; requires high humidity and good air circulation; multiple spikes produced by established plants

Vanda Amphai × Vanda Chiengmai Gold 'Yellow'

BLOOM: 3- to 4-inch diameter; yellow; pink to red spotting and netting; 4 to 10 per spike
GROWTH HABIT: Epiphyte; monopodial
LIGHT REQUIREMENT: High
TEMPERATURE REQUIREMENT: Intermediate to warm
ATTRIBUTES: Intricate pattern; pastel colors

Vanda coerulea

BLOOM: 3- to 5-inch diameter; purple to blue with netted pattern; pale to dark; 5 to 15 per spike
GROWTH HABIT: Epiphyte; monopodial
LIGHT REQUIREMENT: High
TEMPERATURE REQUIREMENT: Intermediate to warm
ATTRIBUTES: Fragrant; long-lasting bloom

Vanda lamellata var. boxallii 'Tom Ritter'

BLOOM: 1- to 2-inch diameter; cream with
reddish-brown splotches; magenta lip;
10 to 25 per spike
GROWTH HABIT: Epiphyte; monopodial
LIGHT REQUIREMENT: High
TEMPERATURE REQUIREMENT: Warm
ATTRIBUTES: Fragrant; long-lasting bloom

Vandachostylis Thailand 'Blue Lightning'

BLOOM: 2-inch diameter; pink, purple, or blue;
darker lip; 5 to 20 per spike
GROWTH HABIT: Epiphyte; monopodial
LIGHT REQUIREMENT: High
TEMPERATURE REQUIREMENT: Cool to warm
ATTRIBUTES: Long-lasting bloom; more than one
spike may be produced simultaneously

Vascostylis Pine Rivers

BLOOM: 2-inch diameter; pink or purple;
10 to 30 per spike
GROWTH HABIT: Epiphyte; monopodial
LIGHT REQUIREMENT: High
TEMPERATURE REQUIREMENT: Cool to warm
ATTRIBUTES: Long-lasting bloom; drought-tolerant

Vascostylis Viboon Velvet

BLOOM: 2- to 3-inch diameter; white to pale purple;
deep purple lip; 5 to 15 per spike; fragrant
GROWTH HABIT: Epiphyte; monopodial
LIGHT REQUIREMENT: High
TEMPERATURE REQUIREMENT: Intermediate to
warm
ATTRIBUTES: Multiple spikes per plant; repeat bloom

Special interest orchids

Some orchids are so exceptional they deserve special mention. The orchids in this section are especially valued for unique characteristics: strong fragrance, unique color combinations, historical significance, or long-lasting bloom.

Angraecum sesquipidale

BLOOM: White to cream flowers, 3 to 4 inches in diameter, are succulent, strongly fragrant at night, and shaped like stars. The spur at the back of the flower can be 12 inches long. Flowers are produced on short spikes, each holding one to several blooms. Flowers are shorter than the surrounding foliage, but stand out clearly among the leaves due to their size, color, and fragrance. Each lasts 4 to 6 weeks.

GROWTH HABIT: This is a drought-tolerant, epiphytic, monopodial orchid. Foliage is slim, straplike, and stiff, with thick, waxy cuticles. Because it can grow quite large it isn't suited to small-space growing on apartment windowsills.

LIGHT REQUIREMENT: High

TEMPERATURE REQUIREMENT: Warm

MATURE SIZE, INCHES: 10 to 30

COMMENTS: The historical significance of this orchid (see Chapter 1) is fascinating. Combined with its outstanding nighttime fragrance and general ease of culture, *Angcm. sesquipidale* is a must for the serious collector. Because this orchid requires high light and temperatures, it grows best in a greenhouse either mounted on a bark slab or potted in a medium- to coarse-grain mix.

Bifrenaria harrisoniae 'Hebrita'

BLOOM: Creamy-white, 3-inch-wide flowers have a waxy sheen and sport a reddish, fuzzy lip with a yellow center. They are strongly fragrant. Short bloom spikes (2 to 3 inches) emerge from the base of the pseudobulbs and bear 1 to 3 flowers at the base of the foliage. A single pseudobulb may produce two bloom spikes.

GROWTH HABIT: Ridged pseudobulbs each produce a single leaf on this sympodial orchid. The pseudobulbs are noticeably yellow compared with the foliage. In nature this orchid may grow either as a lithophyte or as an epiphyte.

LIGHT REQUIREMENT: Medium to high

TEMPERATURE REQUIREMENT: Intermediate to warm

MATURE SIZE, INCHES: 8 to 12

COMMENTS: *Bif. harrisoniae* does not appreciate having its roots disturbed. Grow it as a mounted specimen or in medium-grain bark mix in an orchid basket where frequent watering will be balanced by quick drainage and good air circulation. The fruit-scented flowers last up to 6 weeks. This orchid flowers easily when given adequate light. For best bloom, reduce watering from autumn through spring, giving only enough to keep pseudobulbs from shriveling. It appreciates high humidity year-round.

Bulbophyllum dearei

BLOOM: Showy large (3- to 4-inch) yellow flowers have an unusual shape. Two side sepals arc backwards in a swan dive, while two bottom sepals, shaped like sickles, curve inward to the top sepal, framing a pronounced lip. Both the lip and bottom sepals are strongly streaked with maroon. Flowers may be fragrant and are borne singly on spikes 4 to 7 inches long.

GROWTH HABIT: This sympodial epiphyte produces one leaf from each pseudobulb. During summer's active growth it requires more water than many epiphytes: daily for mounted species and two to three times per week for potted plants.

LIGHT REQUIREMENT: Medium

TEMPERATURE REQUIREMENT: Intermediate to warm

MATURE SIZE, INCHES: 8

COMMENTS: The lips of *Bulbophyllum* orchids are flexible. When a pollinating insect lands on the lip, it loses its balance and tips inward, bumping up against the pollinia. *Bulb. dearei* is a compact plant that grows best in a shallow pot or basket of coarse-grain bark mix or as a mounted specimen. Plants languish after repotting, and may take several months to recover. Otherwise this is an easy-to-grow orchid with outstanding, unique blooms.

Cattleya cernua

BLOOM: Bright vermilion flowers, 1 to 2 inches in diameter and held in clusters of 4 to 7 blooms, make this a showy plant. Each flower reveals a flush of yellow on the lip. This species is often used for its outstanding color in hybridizing minicatts.

GROWTH HABIT: In nature this tiny epiphyte grows flat against tree trunks, with small (1 to 2 inches long) succulent leaves hiding small, flat pseudobulbs.

LIGHT REQUIREMENT: Medium to high

TEMPERATURE REQUIREMENT: Intermediate to warm

MATURE SIZE, INCHES: 3

COMMENTS: For years this plant was known as *Sophronitis cernua*, and chances are good you'll still find it labeled for sale that way. It isn't the easiest orchid to grow, but its outstanding beauty makes it worth a try for growers with a little experience. This orchid tolerates household temperatures better than most orchids formerly known as *Sophronitis*. It grows best as a specimen mounted on a slab and should be allowed to dry out slightly between waterings. Its miniature stature makes it a good candidate for growing under lights, especially if you have an HID setup and can monitor the nighttime temperature drop. Excellent air circulation is required, so consider installing a small fan nearby.

Coelogyne mooreana 'Brockhurst'

BLOOM: As the winner of a First Class Certificate from the American Orchid Society, *Coelogyne mooreana* 'Brockhurst' is an exceptional plant and highly collectible. Three to 10 bright white, 3- to 4-inch fragrant blooms are produced on an upright bloom spike up to 20 inches long. Each flower has an attractive yellow-orange throat. The plant may bloom several times a year.

GROWTH HABIT: This sympodial epiphyte has pseudobulbs 3 to 4 inches long that each produce two thick, shiny leaves.

LIGHT REQUIREMENT: Medium

TEMPERATURE REQUIREMENT: Cool

MATURE SIZE, INCHES: 12 to 18

COMMENTS: *Coel. mooreana* 'Brockhurst' has specific cultural needs: cool temperatures, a winter rest with little water, and high humidity year-round. If you can provide these conditions, this orchid blooms freely and easily, rewarding you with large, fragrant flowers. It is sensitive to repotting so disturb its roots as seldom as possible. Grow it as a specimen mounted on a slab, or in a coarse-grain bark mix that won't biodegrade quickly.

Dendrobium kingianum

BLOOM: The flowers are small and abundant, ½ to 2 inches wide. Enticingly fragrant, they're held 6 to 8 inches above the foliage, forming a cloud of blooms. Individual flowers are triangular, curved in toward the center, and some have an attractively patterned lip. Blooms of straight species are pink and white, although the shade varies from plant to plant. Recent hybrids boost the color palette to include purples, yellows, and reds.

GROWTH HABIT: In nature, this orchid is most often lithophytic, occasionally epiphytic. It is a sympodial, drought-tolerant orchid with slim, upright canes that frequently produce keikis. This is an evergreen dendrobium. Its height is widely variable.

LIGHT REQUIREMENT: Medium to high

TEMPERATURE REQUIREMENT: Cool to intermediate

MATURE SIZE, INCHES: 3 to 20

COMMENTS: A large specimen of *Den. kingianum* looks spectacular in bloom, so let your plant grow rather than dividing it frequently. It grows best in a coarse-grain mix. Best bloom is produced by withholding water in fall and keeping it at about 50°F. The easiest way to achieve this may be to move your plant outdoors in May and back inside right before the first frost. When buds appear, begin watering and bring it back to intermediate temperatures.

Encyclia cordigera

BLOOM: Strongly fragrant and lasting several months, the multicolored flowers of this orchid are unusual in both shape and color combination. They are 2 inches wide with five purple and yellow-green sepals and petals arranged in a star. A large, flared lip emerges from the bottom of the star. The tips of the petals and sepals curl into the center of the flower. The lip may be magenta or white with a magenta spot at the top, depending on the cultivar. Blooms are held on branching spikes, several inches above the foliage.

GROWTH HABIT: This sympodial epiphyte has smooth, shiny pseudobulbs the size of small onions. They form a tight cluster, and bloom spikes emerge from the base of these pseudobulbs.

LIGHT REQUIREMENT: Medium to high

TEMPERATURE REQUIREMENT: Intermediate to warm

MATURE SIZE, INCHES: 15

COMMENTS: The outstanding fragrance and long duration of bloom make this a must-have orchid. Plants grow best in coarse-grain bark in orchid pots or baskets, or as mounted specimens. *E. cordigera* was previously sold as *E. atropurpureum* and may still be found labeled that way. This is an easy and rewarding orchid to grow and bloom.

Gongora bufonia

BLOOM: Cream flowers are speckled with an intricate pattern of dusky rose. Fragrant blooms 2 inches wide are held upside down on pendent bloom spikes that can be up to 30 inches long. Each spike produces several to many flowers. The unusual bloom shape mimics a hovering insect: Its lateral sepals extend up and out like wings, and the orchid lip resembles the head of a pollinating bee.

GROWTH HABIT: This sympodial epiphyte has pseudobulbs that each produce two thin leaves. It requires high humidity year-round. Flower spikes emerge from the base of the pseudobulb and curve downward, holding the blooms below the foliage.

LIGHT REQUIREMENT: Medium

TEMPERATURE REQUIREMENT: Intermediate to warm

MATURE SIZE, INCHES: 12

COMMENTS: These orchids look best when hung so the pendent flowers can be admired. Grow them in orchid baskets or as specimens mounted on slabs. *Gga. bufonia* does not require dormancy.

Lycaste skinneri

BLOOM: Pink or white fragrant flowers are showy, with a dark pink lip. They are large—6 to 7 inches across—and have a triangular shape. Blooms are produced singly on stems up to 12 inches long.

GROWTH HABIT: In nature this sympodial orchid is epiphytic or lithophytic. Ribbed pseudobulbs are tightly clustered and produce two kinds of leaves: large, pleated, thin primary leaves, and small secondary leaves that surround the pseudobulb as it grows. Both types of leaves are deciduous. The small leaves fall away when the pseudobulb finishes expanding and the large leaves are shed when flowering is complete. These orchids are large when fully leafed out and require high humidity during active growth.

LIGHT REQUIREMENT: Low to medium

TEMPERATURE REQUIREMENT: Cool to intermediate

MATURE SIZE, INCHES: 24

COMMENTS: This orchid is best suited to greenhouse growing where it can get the high humidity and growing space it requires. It's a fast-growing orchid and may need repotting every year. Grow it in a fine-grain bark mix and a slatted basket or shallow pot. Authorities disagree on the accepted name for this orchid. You may also find it labeled *Lyc. virginalis*. Either way, this is a spectacular orchid when in bloom.

Maxillariella tenuifolia

BLOOM: *Maxillariella tenuifolia* is also known as the coconut orchid because of its intense coconut scent. Flowers are small—1 to 2 inches—and triangular. Its sepals are dark orange-red with yellow undersides and, depending on the cultivar, a white or yellow lip speckled in red. Blooms, partially hidden among the foliage, are borne singly on short spikes approximately 2 inches long emerging from the base of pseudobulbs. It's not unusual to notice the bloom's scent before you see the subtle flower.

GROWTH HABIT: This orchid is a sympodial epiphyte with an unusual growth habit. Each smooth, oval pseudobulb is borne slightly higher than the preceding pseudobulb, producing a staircase effect. Pseudobulbs produce stiff, grasslike leaves.

LIGHT REQUIREMENT: Medium

TEMPERATURE REQUIREMENT: Intermediate

MATURE SIZE, INCHES: 10

COMMENTS: *Mxl. tenuifolia* should dry out between waterings, but don't let the pseudobulbs shrivel. It requires the fast drainage from a coarse-grain bark mix or bark mounting. You may need to water every one to three days, depending on your potting medium. It grows well under artificial light and is a rewarding, easy orchid.

Paphiopedilum malipoense 'Edmond Oliver'

BLOOM: The unusual combination of pale green flowers striped with deep red make this a visually fascinating flower. Add a fruity perfume and you have a collector's item. Flowers are about 3½ inches in diameter and borne singly on stems 10 to 18 inches tall.

GROWTH HABIT: This is a sympodial terrestrial orchid that tolerates a wide temperature range. In its natural habitat it receives summer daytime temperatures of 80°F and nighttime winter temperatures in the 40s. In cultivation, give this orchid dry, cool winter conditions. Mottled foliage makes this an attractive plant even when it's not in bloom.

LIGHT REQUIREMENT: Low to medium

TEMPERATURE REQUIREMENT: Intermediate

MATURE SIZE, INCHES: 4 to 6

COMMENTS: This orchid was discovered in China in 1984. Its unusual color combination makes it valuable on its own and as a parent for hybrids. The inflorescence is slow to develop from bud to bloom, so be patient. The bud may appear in fall and finally bloom in late winter or spring. *Paph. malipoense* grows best with high humidity in a fine-grain bark mix.

Phaius tankervilleae

BLOOM: Four-foot bloom stalks bear 10 to 20 showy flowers, each 4 inches wide. Sepals and petals are yellow to rusty brown in front and white or yellow in back. All have a strong pink-maroon tubular lip with a ruffled bottom edge. Flowers last for 4 to 6 weeks and may be fragrant. It's not unusual for a single plant to produce more than one bloom spike at a time.

GROWTH HABIT: This sympodial terrestrial orchid has large pseudobulbs (2 to 8 inches tall) that produce large, thin leaves with strong lateral grooves. It requires liberal watering during active growth and needs excellent drainage.

LIGHT REQUIREMENT: Low to medium

TEMPERATURE REQUIREMENT: Intermediate to warm

MATURE SIZE, INCHES: 36 to 40

COMMENTS: Members of the genus *Phaius* can be propagated in an unusual way. When the blooms have died, cut away the section of stem between the pseudobulb and the lowest flower. Lay the stem on a bed of moist sphagnum moss, covering each end to prevent drying. The buds along the stem may each produce a new plant that can be separated from the stem once it has produced several roots. This is a large, impressive orchid. Grow it in a fine-grain bark mix or a combination of fine bark mix and soilless potting mix.

Sarcochilus fitzgeraldii

BLOOM: Showy, succulent white or pink flowers are strongly speckled with red at the center. Each fragrant bloom has a contrasting yellow lip. Up to 15 flowers, each 1 to 1½ inches in diameter, are held on pendent stems 8 to 10 inches long. A single plant may produce more than one bloom spike at a time.

GROWTH HABIT: This monopodial lithophyte has fleshy linear leaves approximately 10 inches long. It has a creeping growth habit and in nature is found in the moist shade of rocky ravines. It grows best with high humidity and strong air circulation.

LIGHT REQUIREMENT: Low to medium

TEMPERATURE REQUIREMENT: Intermediate to cool

MATURE SIZE, INCHES: 4 to 6

COMMENTS: Grow this orchid in a coarse-grain bark mix and a shallow clay pot. Providing winter nighttime temperatures of 45 to 55°F is the key to flower production. If you can accomplish that, you'll be rewarded with plentiful bloom in an outstanding color scheme. *Sarco.* Fitzhart is a popular hybrid of *Sarco. fitzgeraldii* and *Sarco. hartmannii*. It has slightly larger flowers and is generally considered easier to bloom than the straight species.

Vanilla planifolia

BLOOM: Yellow-green flowers, 2½ inches wide, have a hairy yellow lip. Blooms are borne on multiflowered stems 2 to 3 inches long. Flowers open in succession and, once pollinated, produce long, fleshy, fragrant seed capsules 5 to 12 inches long. When cured, these are vanilla beans.

GROWTH HABIT: This monopodial orchid begins life as a terrestrial plant, then quickly climbs up over trees and rocks, rooting at the nodes where it makes contact with an appropriate surface. In nature, this vine can grow to be 100 feet long. In a home or greenhouse it requires high humidity and a sturdy trellis or pole for support. Succulent, leathery leaves are 6 to 8 inches long. The thick green stems are photosynthetic. On most plants, only the leaves photosynthesize, but on specially adapted plants, other parts can also photosynthesize.

LIGHT REQUIREMENT: Medium

TEMPERATURE REQUIREMENT: Intermediate to warm

MATURE SIZE, INCHES: Indeterminate vine

COMMENTS: Although chances are slim you'll actually harvest, cure, and eat pods from your *Vl. planifolia*, it's nice to know you could. This orchid is best suited to a sunroom or greenhouse where it can be allowed to grow up and around, since it doesn't usually flower until it becomes quite long. It blooms best when allowed to scramble horizontally. Pot it in a medium-grain bark mix.

Warczewiczella amazonica

BLOOM: Three-inch single flowers are borne on spikes 6 to 8 inches long. The spikes curve downward under the weight of large blooms. Older plants may produce several spikes at a time, and the orchid can bloom several times a year. Blooms are bright white with thin purple stripes on the lip and have a mild, sweet scent.

GROWTH HABIT: *W. amazonica* is a petite sympodial, epiphytic orchid with no pseudobulbs and thin foliage.

LIGHT REQUIREMENT: Low to medium

TEMPERATURE REQUIREMENT: Intermediate

MATURE SIZE, INCHES: 6 to 8

COMMENTS: Until recently, this orchid was known as *Cochleanthes amazonica.* You'll most likely still find it labeled for sale that way. Its flowers are outstanding and large in proportion to the rest of the plant. It is not drought-tolerant and requires both high humidity and frequent watering. If new leaves emerge looking pleated, this signifies drought, and you should increase watering frequency. It grows best in a fine-grain bark mix and grows well under lights. Its small stature makes it easy to fit into almost any home.

Zygopetalum maculatum

BLOOM: Two- to 3-inch flowers are borne on multibloom spikes that can be 12 to 24 inches long. The petals are greenish-yellow, banded with maroon, and the lip is white with blue-purple stripes, shaped like a fan. Blooms are highly fragrant; a single plant can perfume an entire room.

GROWTH HABIT: *Z. maculatum* is a sympodial epiphyte with prominent pseudobulbs. Its foliage is thin and prone to black spotting when standing water is allowed to accumulate on the leaves. Avoid misting this orchid. It requires high humidity and should be grown on dry wells.

LIGHT REQUIREMENT: Medium to high

TEMPERATURE REQUIREMENT: Intermediate

MATURE SIZE, INCHES: 18 to 24

COMMENTS: This orchid is sometimes sold as *Z. mackayi.* It grows best in fine- to medium-grain bark mix and shallow containers. Recent hybridization has produced many *Zygopetalum* hybrids with even more saturated colors, often emphasizing the blue-purple color of the prominent lips. It's an easy orchid for home growers, and the perfume is outstanding.

Resources

There are orchid clubs and groups all over the world

organized around geographical locations and types of orchids. You may decide to join a local club that meets in person once a month or you may become an active member of a Web-based orchid community. Garden centers, big-box stores, community centers, and adult education programs also offer classes about orchids. All of these resources provide excellent ways to learn how to handle your orchids like a pro, and offer you a chance to meet others who share your interests and who are eager to answer questions.

American Orchid Society

The American Orchid Society (AOS) is a great place to start. Located in Delray Beach, Florida, the AOS has display gardens and a large orchid bookstore. At its headquarters and online, the AOS offers classes, recommends speakers for special events, and sponsors children's programs.

Membership is reasonably priced, and the benefits make it a good value. You get Web access to articles and videos on a wide range of orchid-related topics (repotting, propagation, growing under lights, and so on) plus *Orchids*, a monthly full-color magazine; discount admissions to various botanical gardens; an annual, global listing of orchid suppliers; and links to affiliated societies around the world.

Check out some of the free information available on the AOS website (*aos.org*). If you like what you see, you can join the national society, then check the list of affiliated societies to find a local group to supplement your research with personal contact.

Above: **Learn more about orchids by visiting a display at an orchid show.**

Opposite: **Many orchid shows include plant sales from vendors, which can be a good way to find unusual varieties.**

Orchid organizations

Maybe you've fallen in love with a specific kind of orchid. Are you devoted to phalaenopsis or obsessed with phragmipediums? There are societies dedicated to specific species. This is just the tip of the iceberg. There are Web groups and forums for every type of orchid enthusiast, and many of them have local chapters.

Local orchid clubs and societies usually meet once a month. Meetings begin with a show-and-tell, giving members a chance to bring in and show off their current triumphs. It's an excellent opportunity for new growers to ask questions about specific plants and problems. Each meeting also features a speaker on a topic relevant to home orchid growing. Many orchid societies allow potential members to try out a meeting before paying a fee. It's a good way to see how you'll fit in with your fellow hobbyists. Clubs list local events, offer hands-on workshops, provide opportunities to buy specialized growing supplies, and give you a chance to learn from people who share similar growing conditions.

CYMBIDIUM SOCIETY OF AMERICA
cymbidium.org
GENERAL INTEREST
orchidboard.com
orchidwire.com
forums2.gardenweb.com/forums/orchids
INTERNATIONAL PHALAENOPSIS ALLIANCE
phal.org
PLEUROTHALLID ALLIANCE
pleurothallids.com
SLIPPER ORCHID ALLIANCE
slipperorchid.org

Orchid shows and botanical gardens

Check your local botanical garden for orchid shows during the winter months, plus classes, workshops, and plant sales. Even if you don't have a botanical garden in your area, you may have access to an orchid show. They're big business and an opportunity for growers from around the world to meet their target audience. These public gardens have excellent displays.

ATLANTA BOTANICAL GARDEN
1345 Piedmont Ave. NE
Atlanta, GA 30309
404/876-5859
atlantabotanicalgarden.org

CHICAGO BOTANIC GARDEN
1000 Lake Cook Rd.
Glencoe, IL 60022
847/835-5440
chicagobotanic.org

CLEVELAND BOTANICAL GARDEN
11030 East Blvd.
Cleveland, Ohio 44106
888/853-7091
cbgarden.org

LONGWOOD GARDENS
1001 Longwood Rd.
Kennett Square, PA 19348
610/388-1000
longwoodgardens.org

MISSOURI BOTANICAL GARDEN
4344 Shaw Blvd.
St. Louis, MO 63110
314/577-5100
mobot.org

THE NEW YORK BOTANICAL GARDEN
2900 Southern Blvd.
Bronx, NY 10458-5126
718/817-8700
nybg.org

Mail-order sources

If you don't have a nursery or garden center nearby, there are many online purveyors of orchid supplies. While you're shopping, treat yourself to some bark slabs and HID lighting. Here are a few of the sources you can check.

ANDY'S ORCHIDS
734 Ocean View Ave.
Encinitas, CA 92024
888/514-2639
andysorchids.com

CAL-ORCHID
1251 Orchid Dr.
Santa Barbara, CA 93111
805/967-1312
calorchid.com

CARTER & HOLMES ORCHIDS
629 Mendenhall Rd.
P.O. Box 668
Newberry, SC 29108
803/276-0579
carterandholmes.com

CHARLEY'S GREENHOUSE & GARDEN
17979 State Route 536
Mount Vernon, WA 98273
800/322-4707
charleysgreenhouse.com

GARDENER'S SUPPLY COMPANY
128 Intervale Rd.
Burlington, VT 05401
802/660-3505
gardeners.com

J & L ORCHIDS
20 Sherwood Rd.
Easton, CT 06612
203/261-3772
jandlorchids.com

OAK HILL GARDENS
37W550 Binnie Rd.
P.O. Box 25
Dundee, IL 60118
847/428-8500
oakhillgardens.com

ODOM'S ORCHIDS
1611 South Jenkins Rd.
Fort Pierce, FL 34947
772/467-1386
odoms.com

OFE INTERNATIONAL
12100 S.W. 129th Ct.
Miami, FL 33186
888/633-4685
ofe-intl.com

ORCHIDWEB
4630 Fernbrook Ln. N.
Plymouth MN 55446
800/669-6006
orchidweb.com

PARKSIDE ORCHID NURSERY
2503 Mountainview Dr.
Ottsville, PA 18942
610/847-8039
parksideorchids.com

SANTA BARBARA ORCHID ESTATE
1250 Orchid Dr.
Santa Barbara, CA 93111
805/967-1284
sborchid.com

TINDARA ORCHIDS
30 Spofford St.
Georgetown, MA 01833
978/697-9746
tindaraorchids.com

Online information

Nothing beats an old-fashioned book, except maybe the endless, ever-changing, full-color, free-of-charge resources of the Internet. You can order plants and supplies, examine photos, exchange information in chat rooms, and do solid research. The constantly changing taxonomy of the orchid family is hard to keep up with. Before the age of updatable databases, orchid growers had to wait for new lists to be published in books or magazines. Now, anyone can check online lists for correct plant names and keep up with new hybrids almost as soon as they are registered. Many of these resources are free of charge.

The Royal Horticultural Society in London provides several important tools. Listed below are several informational websites maintained by the RHS:

NEWLY REGISTERED HYBRIDS
Quarterly Supplement to the
International Register of Orchid Hybrids
rhs.org.uk/Plants/RHS-Publications/Orchid-hybrid-lists

ORCHID GENERA LIST OF ABBREVIATIONS
rhs.org.uk/Plants/Plant-science/Plant-registration-forms/
orchidabbrev

ORCHID GENERA AND THEIR COMPONENTS
rhs.org.uk/Plants/Plant-science/Plant-registration-forms/
orchidgenus

PARENTAGE OF ORCHID HYBRIDS
AND THE VALIDITY OF A REGISTERED GREX
The International Orchid Register
apps.rhs.org.uk/horticulturaldatabase/orchidregister/
orchidregister.asp

Kew Royal Botanic Gardens maintains a world checklist of selected plants:
apps.kew.org/wcsp/home.do

Several botanical institutions maintain a world checklist of all accepted species, including orchid genera:
theplantlist.org/browse/A/Orchidaceae/

The Orchid Mall is a giant agglomeration of information on speakers, suppliers, events, and orchid culture:
orchidmall.com

Orchid Species Culture offers culture sheets for hundreds of orchids with recommendations on temperature, fertilizer, potting media, and light, along with detailed plant descriptions and data on native habitat, all for a small fee:
orchidculture.com

OrchidWiz is a digital database updated regularly to incorporate taxonomical changes and new hybrids. It's only available for PCs but you can download a free tutorial. This is a tool for the serious orchid grower. A more affordable version, OrchidWiz Light, is in the works for home orchid growers. orchidwiz.com

Looking for more
gardening inspiration?

See what the experts at
Better Homes and Gardens have to offer.

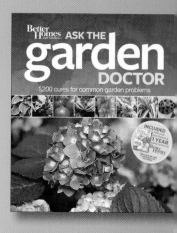

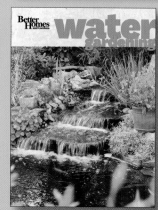

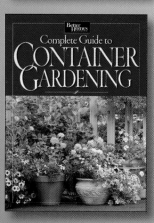

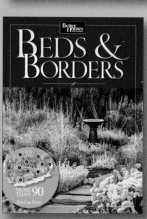

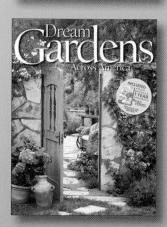

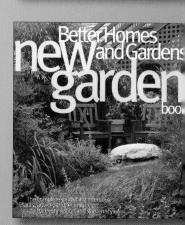

Available where all great books are sold.